RUNNING
TIDE

RUNNING
TIDE ────────────

by Joan Benoit
with Sally Baker

Alfred A. Knopf

New York   1987 ────────────────────

Copyright © 1987 by Joan Benoit Samuelson
All rights reserved under International and Pan-American
Copyright Conventions. Published in the United States by
Alfred A. Knopf, Inc., New York, and simultaneously in
Canada by Random House of Canada Limited, Toronto.
Distributed by Random House, Inc., New York.

Library of Congress Cataloging-in-Publication Data

Benoit, Joan.
Running tide.

1. Benoit, Joan.   2. Runners (Sports)—United
States—Biography.   3. Women athletes—United States—
Biography.   4. Marathon running.   5. Olympic Games
(23rd : 1984 : Los Angeles, Calif.)   I. Baker, Sally.
II. Title.
GV1061.15.B46A3 1987   796.4'26 [B]   86-46318
ISBN 0-394-55457-4

Manufactured in the United States of America
First Edition

To Scott,
whose loving spirit and spunk
have lifted me higher than any victory

ACKNOWLEDGMENTS

Although my editors never took the idea seriously, I wanted to title this book *Out on a Limp*. This would not only describe my body's physical condition after fourteen years of concentrated long-distance running but also help to express my gratitude to the many, many people who took a chance on me. Some consider my sport to be a lonely one, but those who understand running and sport will also understand that this book would simply not exist if it weren't for the countless others in my sport.

My parents' unyielding and unselfish love has always been abundant. Here, finally, is the straight story they have always demanded of me. My family and many friends have always kept me honest and buoyant in the rising and falling tides of life.

Most gracious thanks are extended to Nike, Inc., which took a chance with me early in my career and has treated me like family ever since.

This book is a testament to the patience and perseverance of Sally Baker, who has always known me as a person first and as a runner only in a footnote.

Howard Willman at *Track and Field News* and Chuck Galford of Nike were instrumental in running down the details of my record. Thank heaven they didn't take the chance that I would have kept track of such information.

There are countless others who encouraged me to reach just a little deeper in each race. Race directors, volunteers, and the strong pulse of the running community have all contributed to my development. As we say in Maine, they are "the finest kind."

Finally, a big hug to Dr. Robert E. Leach and Dr. Stan James. Without their help this book would be only a fairy tale.

J.B.S.

April 1987

RUNNING
TIDE

PROLOGUE

I won't forget that raw afternoon in 1973.

I stood at the top of the Main Slope at Pleasant Mountain in Maine. I had been practicing for hours on this slalom course and wanted one last try at a perfect run. I was a tired fifteen-year-old and the light on the mountain was flat, but I pushed myself to ski.

I lost my concentration on the middle of the course and forgot which way I was supposed to be turning into a gate. I rammed the gate and heard my leg break. There was pain, but my scream was more out of surprise and frustration.

People jumped off the T-bar lift and came running when they heard me yell. Looking at them, I tried to take my mind away from my leg by imagining they were dominoes falling in a neat line.

My brother Andy reached me first. He had been watching from the top of the course. He tried to comfort me, saying that the leg might not be broken after all. But I experienced a peculiar sense of knowledge lying in the snow. The leg was broken for sure. I have felt that way only once since then: five weeks before the 1984 Olympic Marathon trials my knee stopped moving and I knew, certainly, that something serious had happened. In neither case was it the pain that revealed the truth; it was a calm, persistent message from somewhere inside my head.

I was taken down the slope on a ski patrol toboggan. Thankfully, nobody said what I was thinking: that it wouldn't have happened if I had only given in to fatigue and quit for the day. My father met us at the bottom of the mountain and took me to a local hospital. I was given a shot of morphine and loaded into the backseat of our station wagon for the hour-long drive to the Maine Medical Center in Portland.

I had gone to bed the night before planning to shower and wash my hair in the morning, but an overnight snowfall meant we had to get going early. So my hair was already dirty when I started out, and after a day of skiing it was filthy. My sole concern at the Maine Medical Center was that no one should see my hair. I tried to keep my ski hat on during the whole procedure, but it was removed. I imagined the doctor and nurse at the emergency room desk chuckling about the greasy-haired teenager.

I was fully sedated while my leg was set. I had expected some anesthesia, but was surprised to find myself waking up in a strange room several hours later. The doctor was leaning over me as I opened my eyes. He asked me typical questions: how did I feel, what was my name, etc. I answered him by saying "Thanks for fixing me!" and trying to jump out of bed. In the mist of anesthesia my only thought was that he'd put my leg back into working order. He convinced me otherwise and I settled back until the doctor let my father take me home.

The broken leg was the last thing I needed. I had hoped to climb into the "A" ranks of ski racing and there were other things on my schedule that winter. I wanted to get an early start on preparations for the spring track season. Most of all,

I wanted to get my driver's license: my exam was set for the following week.

I wondered if there wasn't some sort of compensation for my mishap. I had spent the whole weekend worrying over a paper I was supposed to write on Edith Hamilton's *Mythology*. I was thinking about that paper as I took my final run down the mountain. I didn't know where I would find the energy to write it after such a long day. Usually my schoolwork came first, but this was a rare occasion when I had put something off for too long. Now I had an excuse for an extension. I smiled for the first time since the accident.

I stayed away from school for a couple of days and did a good job on Edith Hamilton. If I had a favorite season in those days—and it is difficult to choose a favorite in Maine, since all four have something wonderful to offer—it was winter. So it was maddening, but I had to learn to live with the inactivity. I tacked a couple of cardboard signs to my bedroom door, reading "Stamp Out Summer" and "Half Fast Skier."

On my first day back at school I tried to sneak into biology class behind a crowd of students because I didn't want the teacher to ask what happened to my leg. Unfortunately, I was not yet graceful on my crutches, so I bumbled into the room and took my seat noisily. Nobody said anything as I pretended to be fully occupied in finding a pencil and my biology notebook.

The teacher, Keith Weatherbie, was also the coach of the boys' cross-country team, and I had run with them on one occasion the previous fall. He expected a great deal from his athletes and, to use his favorite metaphor, I already had one strike against me: I was a girl. That's what I thought, anyway. I was sure he'd feel I was a hopeless nerd for breaking my leg. I was also certain he would be upset with me because I had not done my best as an athlete.

Keith introduced me to interval workouts when I was a junior, the season after I broke my leg. He'd picked up the nickname Catfish as a baseball pitcher, so the long workouts were called cat-killers; the shorter ones were mini-killers. Both were well named. A cat-killer consisted of a one-mile run, two half-mile repeats, four quarter-mile repeats, and eight 220-yard repeats. Even when I was a senior a cat-killer could make me drop to the ground, exhausted. Keith would stand over me and say, "Well, it must be time to go home and study," and that would bring me off the ground enraged at myself because I knew I could be doing better on his tests. The fact that I was always trying to impress him, in and out of class, was a great motivator. His style was similar to that of my current adviser, Bob Sevene, who has only to mention someone else's workouts or race results to get me out of a mental slump. Both Bob and Keith are also concerned with the academic preparation of athletes; while coaching at the college level, Bob made sure all of his athletes graduated.

My apprehension over Keith's reaction was wasted. He waited until my classmates had left before he asked about the accident, and he didn't chew me out or kid me. More than anything, I was upset with myself; my picture of a mocking Keith was a convenient vehicle for those feelings of inadequacy I was dragging around along with my cast.

The cast gave me fits until I got it changed for a smaller, lighter, walking version. There were three flights of stairs at school and I had to climb each of them every day. All the hard work involved in just getting around probably kept me in shape for those months, and I had the solace of making high honors twice that year. I normally did my best schoolwork when I had to fit it in with a zillion other activities (excellent training for the life I am leading at the moment), so I was surprised when I found I could use leisure time so well.

There is a belief that I didn't start running until the spring after my skiing accident, but actually I ran track as a freshman under the guidance of Paula Smith and Andrea Cayer. Andrea was the only Cape Elizabeth High School teacher who was shorter than I, and that in itself was an inspiration. But she was also a successful physical education teacher. She had a great rapport with her students as well as with her athletes, and she had been a good high school athlete herself. I felt her experience supported the advice she gave me. Some of my perseverance in athletics stems from the C that Andrea gave me in gymnastics. To get a C in any subject, much less phys ed, was devastating. I tried harder.

That spring I moped around the track after my cast came off. I wanted so much to be involved with the team that I volunteered to rake the long-jump pit during practice and to drag the heavy foam high-jump landing pads from the field to the school building when the team was finished using them.

Running felt horrible at first. A couple of weeks after the cast was removed I decided to take a strengthening run. I wasn't making much progress, but I kept it up for a while. A little boy crossed a nearby field and paused to watch me. He approached when I stopped to rest.

"You shouldn't run when you're limping," he said, shaking his head as he walked by.

It was good advice, but from that day to this I have not heeded it.

The leg was not my first injury and it would not be my last. A cinder in my hand reminds me of the time I dove for the finish line in a 50-yard dash. I carry bumps and scars from a lifetime of competition. My most celebrated injury was a knee that required arthroscopic surgery two weeks before the Olympic Trials. It would not have been so devastating (or so famous) without its poor timing. All athletes get hurt.

Injury, whether physical or emotional, is a personal ordeal. We learn much about ourselves through injury and disappointment; the first time we fall down as children we learn that in order to overcome a force like gravity we must bend our wills to this peculiar harness that binds us.

My response to the lows and highs has been the making of me. My worst races have been my best teachers. Every time I fail I assume I will be a stronger person for it. I keep on running, figuratively and literally, despite a limp that gets more noticeable with each passing season, because for me there has always been a place to go and a terrible urgency to get there. For as long as I can remember I have been setting goals for myself and dealing with the consequences of either meeting or falling short of them. I have tried to accept my setbacks as the will of someone whose judgment I have no right to question. But I also believe that that someone—who, for me, is God—expects me to push against the obstacles with all my strength and to give up only when I am fairly and honestly defeated.

I guess I will eventually experience true success and true failure; I have not met with either yet. The only real failure is the failure to try. Perhaps one day I will find myself unwilling to try; I hope not. But should that day arrive, I will know what failure is. Similarly, it seems to me that real success comes when a person is able to say of one of her accomplishments, "That is a good job well done," and then leave that accomplishment behind. When I run a good race I think about how I might have done better and what I will do next time. True success eludes me, but I may be setting impossible standards for myself. Some day I may have to be satisfied with something less than the goals I set for myself: then and only then will I feel tested.

My skiing injury did lead me to run more, and because of

my affection for running I was able to give up my dream of being a world-class skier. From the beginning of my development as an athlete I've been willing to learn the lessons injury can teach. I didn't surrender my dream lightly; but when I stood on a mountain the following winter and was scared, the realist in me took over. I could no longer hope to be a great skier if I was afraid. But because I ran and played other sports, I could give up competitive skiing; running was compensation.

The goal I can neither reach nor let go of is out there somewhere. I dread meeting it. So until it shows its face I will continue to do what I have always done: I will keep on doing my best.

ONE

Captain John Smith named the town where I was raised. I don't think there were any permanent Indian settlements on the site at that time, so Smith was actually naming a point of land, not a town. I wish I could go back in time for one look at the place he must have seen. Beautiful now, it must have been astonishingly so back then. The story has it that Smith sailed along our coast naming things. I picture him standing uneasily in the bowsprit netting, pointing his finger at various clumps of trees and declaring "You shall be called . . . whatever." Our town was named Cape Elizabeth, after his queen.

My father grew up in the next neighborhood over. His family founded Benoit's, a retail clothing business. My mother is an import from Massachusetts; her father, George Ryan, was city editor at the old Boston *Herald* and wrote a highly respected column called "Top of the Morning."

Both my parents were adventurous young adults. My father took an accelerated course at Bowdoin College and graduated in time to spend most of World War II in the Tenth Mountain Division—the ski troops. Once when I was very young I came upon him sorting through the contents of a battered steel box. He told me his prized possessions were there, so I peered over his shoulder for a good look. He showed me a small leather folder; the surface was cracked with age. Inside was a minuscule piece of paper—even my young eyes had trouble reading what was written on it. It was a prayer my grandmother had given him to carry during the war. I didn't know this was common practice for soldiers; I thought the prayer had been written especially for Dad, that it was God's way of wishing him good luck. Years later, when I read about how dangerous the war was for the ski troops, I thought I wasn't far wrong about that prayer. My father had avoided death from German bullets, exposure to cold, and numerous avalanches.

My mother flouted tradition and went off to William and Mary for her education. Young ladies from Massachusetts who were bound for college were supposed to stay in New England. That William and Mary was coeducational was bad enough, but it was also in the South, practically a foreign country. Mom loved the college and she loved living in another part of the United States. When the trains weren't loaded with soldiers she could visit her brothers at the University of North Carolina. After graduation she continued to surprise the people at home; she joined the American Red Cross and spent the war in India and China.

A mutual friend introduced Mom and Dad to each other at a summer party in Cape Elizabeth. They fell in love and were married when the war was over, and spent their honeymoon in the Laurentians.

My mother wasn't a great skier. She was a talented athlete, but she hadn't spent much time on skis. Dad was an expert. On their honeymoon he ushered Mom onto a chair lift and took her to the top of a difficult trail. She looked down and then looked at my father. He saw she wasn't going to follow him down that mountain and said, "You wait here, dear. I'll take a few quick runs and be right back for you."

The marriage survived anyway.

Andre Jr. was born in 1952; Peter followed eighteen months later. I arrived in 1957, John a year and a half after me. Growing up I felt more allied to John than to the other two boys, but as adults we have all been very close. Andy and Peter never wanted John and me to tag along with them. I resented this treatment at the time and tried to prove I was just as fast, just as tough, and just as fearless as they were.

There was no place for a shrinking violet around my house. My mother taught us the rules of etiquette—"ladies first," and so on—but neither my brothers nor I considered me a lady. If I couldn't beat them to the catcher's mitt, the best sandwich in the ski lunch, or the window seat in the car, too bad. If I had trouble carrying my skis off the mountain at the end of the day, that was cause for a merciless ribbing. They weren't being mean; they were treating me the way I expected to be treated: as an equal. In fact, the one thing they could do to get a rise out of me was try to relegate me to "girl" status. We all knew girls were wimpy.

I sometimes thought my parents treated me differently because I was a girl. One thing I remember best about my early childhood is how much I wanted to go skiing with my parents and the older boys. Every Saturday they would head for a nearby mountain and leave John and me behind with our grandmother. I was older than John and thought I should be taken along.

One Saturday I begged to go. I was three or four and probably about the size of a throw pillow, but I could make a lot of noise. I pleaded and groaned and carried on, but no one paid any attention to me. My parents said I was too young and that was that. I asked if they were being so horrible to me because I was a girl. They said no, very patiently. I was lucky they didn't settle the whole argument with a spanking. No doubt Andy and Peter lorded it over me, making me even more determined. I was sure I could do anything they could do.

In the cellar I found some small skis, the official first pair for every kid in the family. Dad gave them to each of us in turn as the older child outgrew them; he would bring them out for Christmas and put a fresh coat of paint on them. They still showed scars from Peter's use when I discovered them, but even beaten up they were beautiful to me. I strapped them on and tried to ski down our steep front lawn. The experiment was a failure—I fell down several times and was deposited at Grandmother's house as usual. I sucked on black jellybeans all afternoon to console myself.

The next year I went with my family to Sugarloaf Mountain in Kingfield for the first time. There are things about Sugarloaf that I suppose I will still remember if I live a hundred years. It was an imposing sight when I was a child. With no condominiums and few roads at the base, the mountain was a wild, thrilling place. Just driving toward it gave me goosebumps.

For a couple of winters the Benoits and four other families shared an old house near the mountain. The place was small, but by sleeping dormitory-style in the loft everyone could be accommodated. A wood stove was the only source of heat; we burned dowels picked up at a nearby paper mill. The house was always cold, but we children hardly noticed.

The skiing was terrific; I loved it from the beginning. The speed and freedom it gave me were new, welcome sensations. Learning to make the equipment respond to the movements of my legs and arms, learning to keep my balance or fall safely, learning to relish the warmth and hot chocolate in the lodge after a thorough chill: these were the great joys of my young life.

At first I stood between my father's legs—he on his skis and I on mine—hugging his knees as he moved down a gentle slope, trying to feel the rhythm in his movements. At times I almost felt his legs were mine; he made everything look easy. Skiing is bound up in grace and finesse, and my father had both in abundance. After an hour or two with him I knew what I wanted from my own skis.

Of course I expected to get right on and *ski*. I tried, but my skis wouldn't do what Dad's had and I spent most days lying in the snow. Skiing attire in the 1960s was not up to current standards—the damp and cold penetrated quickly despite careful dressing. Underneath my layers of clothing my skin was numb, then painful, from the frequent landings on the snow.

There were other unanticipated problems; for example, I had to learn to ride the T-bar. You are supposed to stand in front of the wooden bar and let it push you to the top of a slope, but since I was too small to hold it down that way, I had to sit on it. People thought I was hilarious. On those few occasions when I didn't fall, I hung on like a monkey, my skis dangling below me.

The other feature of the T-bar I found daunting was that the lift attendants requested it be ridden by people in tandem, meaning that I had to ask strangers to ride with me. I would stand by the lift line for what seemed like an hour, trying to work up the courage to speak to someone. And when I finally did speak, I often got the jokers. "Are you single?" I'd ask, peeping like a bird. "No, I'm married," the joker would say. Very funny.

I persisted despite the trials, fighting the T-bar until I had it beaten. After that it was fun to ride. The best fun of all was to ride alone, if you were coordinated enough to balance the bar without help.

People ask how I can run with pain or keep working toward a goal that seems hopelessly distant. I think back on my early failures with the T-bar. I didn't want to look ridiculous, I didn't want people to laugh at me, and I didn't want to talk to strangers; but I knew if I was going to ski I would have to master the T-bar. If I want to run a marathon faster than I've run in the past, I have to cope with the discomfort that sometimes accompanies long-distance running. I know the end result will be worth the effort. It is too bad that very few T-bars are being installed at ski areas today.

Skiing itself—along with the rituals that accompanied it in my family—was one of my best early teachers. It was a wonderful introduction to sports, but it also taught me about sacrifice, about picking myself up and going on in spite of adversity, and about striving.

I didn't realize I was learning lessons. All I knew was, as long as there was snow on the ground we skied every weekend from November to April. There was more snow when I was a kid than there is now; during the past several winters my skiing has been limited by lack of snowfall. Once in a while I wonder if all the dire predictions some scientists have made about the destruction of our ozone layer are coming true. Perhaps the sun is melting our ice caps, or perhaps we are in the midst of a naturally produced warming trend. For whatever reason, we have less snow, which is frustrating for inveterate skiers like me.

There were priorities ahead of skiing, of course. On Saturday mornings Dad would drop the four of us off for our instruction in C.C.D. (Christian Catholic Doctrine) on his way to work and Mom would pick us up from there and take us to the mountain. If we overslept and had to go to the nine o'clock, rather than the eight o'clock, class, it would be ten before we were on the road and eleven thirty before we were on skis. And not only did we have to show up for class, we had to do the work once we got there.

On Sundays we got up for early mass. Easier said than done, since we were tired after skiing on Saturday. This was Dad's only free day, and he was anxious to get to the slopes. He would rouse us, moving from one child to another until he was reasonably sure we were all awake.

We went to mass in our ski clothes and tried to pay close attention, but the hour was early and the church was quiet; it was difficult not to doze. Recalling those times—and all the Easter Sundays when we felt like second-class citizens because we were in ski clothes and everyone else was decked out—I'm grateful for the institution of the Saturday evening mass in the 1960s. I was finally alert enough to listen to what was going on in church. I might have come to that point of my own accord once I got older, but I liked being able to sit up and take notice as a kid, too. Easter was still hard—you don't go to Easter mass on Saturday—but every year there was an Easter Classic race on the mountain, followed by an Easter egg hunt, so that made up for the feelings of inferiority I'd had in church. In any case, I was sorry for the little girls in their new bonnets. Those hats sported elastic chin bands that cut thin red lines into tender skin. And I was sure my ski boots were more comfortable than the tight patent leather shoes all the other girls wore.

Trying to budget time for skiing around religious obligations helped me form some of the priorities that would shape my later life. The clearest lesson was that there were some things in the universe that came before my interests and desires. God and my parents, for example. Prayer, too. There were times when I thought about skipping my prayers but didn't; they were important.

Skiing was also a physical challenge. Good skiers are somewhat ruthless in their training, forcing themselves to confront difficult trails over and over again until they are mastered. Good skiers ski in all weather. Any snowstorm short of a screeching blizzard found the four Benoit children on the mountain; wind and cold couldn't stop us. We were welcome to retreat to the lodge if we were cold, but there was pride involved in not being the one to leave the slopes first. I'm not sure about the source of that particular competition, but I do know why we were unwilling to complain: our father never groused about anything. Though he may have felt sympathy when we grumbled, he didn't show it in any obvious way. He must have figured we were smart enough to come in out of the cold without his urging. But every one of us hated to admit that anything as paltry as the weather could bring us down. So we shivered and got back on the T-bar for one last run even when we could hardly feel our feet and hands. I think I did some permanent damage to my fingers and toes by ignoring them back then; nowadays I feel the cold in them soon after my first trip down the mountain and I usually have to quit skiing long before I want to. Whatever my body suffered, however, was more than made up for by what I gained in tenacity. If it appears that running in pain doesn't bother me, it's because I learned to manage it when I was a young skier. I found a part of myself which could go on in spite of it and I developed that part.

But I don't want to give the impression that I got up on weekend mornings with the attitude of a stevedore about to spend a tough day on the docks. I loved skiing. Most days the weather was fine, especially in early spring. By March it would begin to get warm and we could ski in shirt sleeves. Then I would relish the feel of the wind dancing through the gaps in my clothes. I sometimes wore goggles, but on sunny days they weren't necessary—the warmth would cover my face like a mask. Skiers had the best, earliest tans in town.

Because I ski, I know why people enjoy driving race cars. Great speed is an opiate, and speed that is under your control, open to your manipulation, is the best high of all. I don't race cars, but barring that, I have yet to find a sport which comes close to skiing for pure exhilaration.

I wasn't surprised, therefore, when I took it into my head to become a world-class skier. I was young—eight or nine—but the goal wasn't set childishly. I didn't want to be a skier one day, a teacher the next, and a doctor the third. Underlying every other ambition I set for myself between those early skiing years and the time I broke my leg was the desire to ski in the Olympics. I knew I would have to train for a career to support myself, and there were many occasions when I faced reality and admitted that pinning my hopes on athletics was irresponsible, but the dream refused to be shunted aside.

I worked with it as well as I could. Fortunately, my ambition was entirely in my own mind. Unlike many child athletes, I was under absolutely no pressure to train. In fact, when I was old enough to baby-sit I had to make money to pay for equipment and ski camp. During vacations from high school I waitressed at the Pleasant Mountain Inn so I would have a place to stay on the mountain. They didn't serve lunch; I could get on the slopes after breakfast and ski until the last bell. Regulars on Pleasant Mountain urged my father to send me away for coaching.

I had my heart set on attending a Vermont ski academy, but after much thought my parents decided not to let me go. My hopes rose again when I learned that a similar academy was to be opened at Sugarloaf. Once again, my parents felt that education came before skiing.

I continued to train on weekends and during school vacations. In junior high I joined an intensive training program at Pleasant Mountain and competed as much as I could. I had begun competition at age ten and always enjoyed it. I won as often as I lost, but .500 wasn't the average I was aiming for. I wanted to win every race: not because I took great pleasure in beating other people, but because I wanted to know I was getting better.

My parents wouldn't let me become as myopic toward life's other concerns as you're supposed to be if you aspire to athletic prowess. Winning was neither everything nor the only thing; it was one of many things. My parents would have laughed uproariously if I'd come to them with fire in my eyes and said, "Mom, Dad, from now on I'm going to train to be a skier and that's it!" They were never insensitive to my desires— I'm sure it hurt them to turn me down on going to ski academy—but there wasn't any room around our house for a Star, either. Mom and Dad were trying to rear four happy, intelligent, useful, loving kids. What we did with the grounding they gave us was our business. They had no intention of pointing us toward careers before we had grown into a sense of ourselves. We were exposed to the widest imaginable variety of pursuits from which to pick and choose. Andy and Peter both love to draw and paint; I took up stamp collecting and had piano lessons; John dabbled successfully in almost everything. None of us viewed life through a tunnel formed by a single, all-consuming passion.

I'll admit I was terribly serious about skiing. Once in a while my father tried to slow me down. I suppose it's hard to see your child place enormous emphasis on any one pursuit, because with the disappointments you've suffered in your life, you know how far she can fall. Parents must walk a tightrope between protecting their children from heartache and encouraging them to develop their talents. Dad was always checking to make sure I thought skiing was worth all the time I was giving to it. When he was satisfied that I was happy, he placed few obstacles in my way.

We did argue over the type of bindings I should use. He wanted me to be safe, so he made me wear a brand that had a guardian angel as its trademark. The slightest pressure on a turn released the binding—time and time again I zoomed into a turn in a race, only to feel my bindings let go. I carried on about it for years. Dad's standard, unbending reply was that safety was more important than winning races. That was easy for him to say, since I, not he, was the one piling up Did Not Finish results.

When I was finally permitted a pair of bindings that hung in there on the turns, I broke my leg. To his credit, Dad didn't say, "I told you so."

I went through the usual crises of adolescence. It is difficult for anyone to develop a sense of herself in junior high school, but of course I felt I was the only one who was different—gawky and shy. I always seemed to have a cold sore on my lip when it was time to take the class picture or deliver an oral report. (I was sure everyone was looking right at my lips.) And if that wasn't bad enough, my clothes were always neat and well tailored, which separated me from the "in" group. In the late 1960s, "neat" and "clean" didn't inspire much admiration in young people. My parents— and, had I only known, most of my friends' parents—stood figuratively at the front door with their arms thrown out at their sides and dared us not to look presentable when we went to school.

Presentability was my father's business. He didn't work

six days a week at the store helping men look stylish so he could come home to a kid in white socks and loafers. He still won't wear white after Labor Day. Once I wrote a composition about the day in spring when men are allowed to change from winter hats to straw hats.

There would be no disheveled hippies in my family.

Besides being oppressively well groomed, I had other worries. For one thing, I was afraid I was far too interested in sports. At an age when my girl friends were coming down out of the trees to wear makeup and exchange brass ID bracelets with boys, I still wanted to ski, skate, and play tennis and baseball. Skiing was acceptable, since lots of cute boys skied. Skating was fine, but only if you had white skates with pink, candy-striped laces. I owned black hockey skates. Tennis was okay, too, if you kept your overhead smash to yourself while the boys were watching. Playing baseball was definitely out: all pickup games were forbidden in the unwritten rulebook of seventh grade.

Everything changed too fast. It seemed that one day we were capturing tadpoles at the pond and putting catkins in our bicycle spokes, and the next day we weren't allowed to play sports unless they were played, if not in uniform, at least in fashionable sport clothes. It was confusing, because there weren't many organized games for girls. We were supposed to wait until high school for the chance to build character by participating in team sports. I still played kickball and baseball with the boys on my street, but would quit when I knew it was time for the neighborhood fathers to return from work. I didn't want people to think I was a tomboy.

I was able, however, to keep up with my favorite sports as well as the new, more acceptable ones. The activity paid off—in junior high I was in the ninety-fourth percentile for fitness according to the criteria used by the President's Council on Physical Fitness and Sports. The teachers told me my rating would be higher if I knew how to breathe properly while running. I eventually got the last laugh on that score; as far as I know, I breathed in the Olympic Marathon the same way I did on the Cape Elizabeth track.

The pleasing moments in junior high, however, were few. I spent most of my time there looking forward to getting out. We had been divided into two academic teams upon entering the seventh grade and most of my friends were on the other team. I made new friends but missed being in classes with people I'd liked since kindergarten. Academically, junior high was difficult. I don't know whether it was my attitude or the zooish atmosphere that made my teachers expect less than my elementary school teachers had, but I could tell they weren't cherishing high hopes for me. My science teacher told my parents I was an average student doing average work and they should be satisfied with that. The implication was that I had left my brain on the side of the road somewhere between sixth and seventh grades. I worked hard at my studies to try to gain back some of the respect I'd lost.

If school was exhausting and somewhat maddening, summertime was blessed. I never missed a day of school between the time my dog bit me when I was in first grade and the day I broke my leg. It did not occur to me to do as my friends did and take a day off when the pressures of being thirteen drove me up a wall. By summertime, therefore, I was really ready for a break. My friend Anne Peabody and I had tennis on our minds. We would play once in the early morning, go to the beach for the day, and play again after supper. This schedule taught me the value of taking two varied workouts each day instead of one long one. You can work harder for shorter periods of time and you end up getting higher-quality exercise. I wish I still had enough time to visit the beach between workouts; I suppose everyone would like to have one more summer as a kid.

One memory I can relive whenever I wish is of my time on the island that was my mother's childhood summer home. We spent two or three weeks there every summer. Now that we are grown, my mother is free to live there from June through September, and she cheerfully leaves everything behind to go. The Island works on her soul, I think—she comes back refreshed and ready to face winter commitments. I try to make several short visits each summer.

I loved the Island because there was so much to do. I got my first good arm muscles from rowing its circumference in an old boat. When I was tired of boating I could always swim, though the water in the middle of Casco Bay is far colder than off the mainland. Swimming from the rocky beach reminds me a bit of standing on top of Sugarloaf in a snowstorm: I wonder just how far I should let the numbness proceed before I retreat. When it was very cold, there were other things to occupy me: digging clams, looking for crabs in tidal pools, watching the lobstermen unload their catches. My brothers and cousins and I had sea-glass stores on opposite ends of our common beach, where we traded the lovely, dull-edged glass that washed up there. We lined the glass up on shelves of rock, one color per shelf, and, though we left it there day and night, it was not disturbed. We pocketed our best pieces to take home at night and bartered for others. Everyone we loved got a sea-glass lamp for Christmas—a clear bottle filled with the precious shards and topped with a light fixture.

Year-round Island residents (there are about a hundred of them) good-naturedly call the out-of-state summer people "dogfish." There is nothing much lower than that in the harbor—it's a fish that grubs around on the ocean floor. We were better than dogfish, being Mainers, but we were set apart nonetheless. To me the Island felt as much like home as home did, and as the years have passed I have been accepted as a "real" Islander.

I hope the people there didn't mind when I immortalized the place for its berries. In the summer we have raspberries, blueberries, and blackberries to pick as they come into season and we have jam all year long. At the press conference following the Olympic Marathon I was asked where I could be found in the coming week. I said, "Look in a berry patch in Maine." They thought I was kidding.

I talk about the Island and its people as much as I do because a part of my personality was formed there. I couldn't miss absorbing some of their quiet, self-effacing ways. I've been thought of as extraordinarily shy, but I don't think I am. What is mistaken for reticence is the Island watchfulness, the attitude that it is better to listen than to talk. The Olympic summer kept me from making a long visit to the Island, where I might have gathered my wits. To be separated from a place I love that much was like being separated from a part of myself. It is the one place where I can completely relax. Nobody can find me there, nobody can call. The closest telephone is at the store near the ferry landing.

My mother spoils me rotten during my visits; she cooks my favorite foods, she is quiet in the morning if I want to sleep, and she does the housework as if it makes her happy. All I have to do is jog the footpath a few times a day, read, sleep, go berrying, and lie in the sun. Once in a great while I am sent to the well for a bucket of water. Hardly the life of a dogfish.

.　　.　　.

The Island, the mountains, the little school I attended, and, especially, my family—these were my nurturers. Within my early experiences were the lessons I needed to prepare me for life as an athlete. I learned to put something besides myself at the center of my universe. That came in handy whenever I tried to feel sorry for myself. I was taught to be tough, to meet challenges without flinching. I was also taught to love myself but strive to be a better person. I learned to value silence and contemplation. I learned how to earn respect. I came away knowing when to laugh.

All before I took a single step as a serious runner.

TWO

*A*thletes who start young in their chosen sport can point to an early determination to excel in that sport alone. Tennis players, swimmers, and gymnasts begin intensive training when they are little more than babies; which is why, I believe, so many of them fall by the wayside so early. If you start working hard at seven, burnout is a real possibility by thirteen or fourteen. Long-distance runners shouldn't begin so early, as they could do permanent harm to developing bones and muscles, so they should experience a variety of sports and pursue other activities. I always knew I wanted to be an athlete because I loved to be active and to compete, but running wasn't a sport I gave much attention to as a child. So I can't look back and trace my primal devotions step by step, backing them up with training logs and competition results. There was no Little League for runners in my hometown and none was needed. A kindergarten teacher remembers that I used to hang on the fringes of the older kids' group in the playground and run away with their kickball when I got a chance. My childhood was filled with athletic endeavors, none of which would mean anything if I hadn't gone on to pursue a career in running.

But a career has to start somewhere, and, as nearly as I can tell, mine started at a gymkana in Norfolk, Connecticut.

It was the summer after my eighth birthday. My brother Peter and I were invited to drive to Norfolk with our aunt and uncle and several cousins. Peter and I would return home on a bus by ourselves. He was eleven and probably very reluctant to look after me, but it was a chance to travel and he grabbed it.

On Saturday the Norfolk country club held its annual gymkana. My cousins were anxious to compete and I was eager to find out what a gymkana was (it sounded like an antelope), so their parents got us to the club early that morning. It slowly dawned on me that a gymkana was basically a track and field competition. Anyone could take part, so I signed up for everything appropriate for my age group.

One of the first events was an 880 for teenaged boys. Because I was small enough to wriggle to the front of the crowd without bothering anyone, I had a good view. Separated from Peter and my cousins, I was able to watch without distraction. I was fascinated. One young man took a quick lead in the race and maintained it to the end. He seemed confident; when he crossed the finish line he was winded, but I could tell he wasn't in as much pain as the other runners.

This race has stayed in my memory so long because I got my first good advice on running while watching it. I was trying to figure out what it was that made the lead runner look so good when a woman behind me said, "You can tell Jim runs for the high school team. Look at the way he carries his arms." Jim kept his arms close to his sides and ran with his elbows tucked in to his waist. His head and upper body hardly moved—he used his energy to power his legs. That was what made him look so good.

I remembered Jim's style when I ran my races later that day. I signed up for five running and two jumping events; holding my arms as the boy had, I won five blue ribbons.

No big deal, I thought, it was fun. My cousins, on the other hand, were none too pleased with my day's work; I couldn't understand why. The ride back to their house was silent. My aunt was mortified: her guest had turned out to be an eight-year-old ringer.

After a time I couldn't stand the silence, so I made the mistake of admiring the red and white ribbons the others had won. I said I thought they were very nice. My cousins hissed at me. "Second place!" they screamed. "Third place! Hon-or-a-ble mention!"

Now I understood. Other people loved to win just as much as I did. Until that day I had not considered the costs of competition. Somebody had to lose. I didn't mind if I lost after doing my best, but I preferred to win and so did everyone else. I have my cousins to thank for an early lesson in the importance of winning with modesty.

The lesson didn't fully take on that day, however. In the evening we had a cookout and my uncle took pictures through the smoke. There I was in my beribboned glory, still the Winner. I should have put the ribbons in my suitcase, but this was my first taste of success and it went to my head. My cousins eventually forgave me, and my aunt found that no one at the club begrudged me anything.

I didn't have another opportunity to compete in a track meet for two years. Not that it mattered; even at this young age I was serious about skiing and played other sports only because they were enjoyable. If anything, running was a means of transportation.

In the spring of 1967, I was in the fourth grade at Cottage Farms School. Only the kids who lived on my end of town were lucky enough to go there: the other elementary school was big and looked like an institution. Cottage Farms resembled an illustration from a book by Louisa May Alcott. We adored the place.

The principal, Reita Andren, was a believer in the education of what is now called the "whole child." She thought our bodies were almost as important as our minds. In accordance with the new guidelines of the President's Council on Physical Fitness and Sports, she set out to encourage each child in the school to excel physically. She announced that we would have a field day, with footraces, jumping competitions, throwing contests, basketball shooting, the works.

I had had a checkered career in physical fitness programs at Cottage Farms. In the first grade I received straight C's for whatever passed for phys ed. The teacher suggested, in the comment section of my report card, that I had trouble with team sports. I did prefer solo activity, but once I knew my teachers were critical of me for that reason I shaped up and got better grades. Nonetheless, our disorganized playground games—kickball, marbles, and dodgeball—were better than any we played under the teachers' supervision.

Field Day was held in the afternoon. We always went home for lunch from Cottage Farms (often getting a much-needed chance to regroup from a bad morning over Mom's soup and kind words), but that day was special. Not only were we to spend the entire afternoon outside in the May sunshine, but the girls were allowed to wear slacks or shorts for the first time ever. It was wonderful. We could dig in and compete without worrying that our underwear would show.

We had a terrific afternoon. I had good reason to be cheery—I was reliving the gymkana. Still holding my arms in imitation of Norfolk Jim, I took first place in several running events. A boy tried to shove me out of the way at the end of the 300-yard dash and ended up pushing me over the finish line ahead of him. Even though I was furious with him I took the opportunity to be a Nice Winner. I didn't tell Mrs. Andren what he'd done.

At the end of the day, despite my success, I came away dissatisfied with myself. Mrs. Andren gave me a Certificate of Achievement in Physical Fitness with four blue stars and I dutifully stuck it in my scrapbook, but I wanted to be the best in everything. The idea that I could have done better obsessed me. I don't know whether I wanted to improve to make myself happy or to impress the teachers—the desire was there and I didn't analyze it.

The following year I was determined to win more ribbons. The event was directly tied to the President's Council fitness tests, so we all had to participate in certain races and competitions. I decided to practice the softball throw, my weakest event by far.

I loved playing baseball and had been anxious to try out for Little League. They told me I was a *girl* in such incredulous tones that I gave up the idea. I had lost some of my ability since the boys walked off our sandlot into their new uniforms: from the moment they entered Little League they refused to play with girls anymore. My throwing arm was in lousy shape and I couldn't seem to bring it back.

The depressing part of practicing was watching my friends Diann Wood and Carl Horner fetch the balls I'd tried so hard to throw and wing them back effortlessly. Di and Carl had the best arms in school, but such was my ambition that I felt I should be able to hurl that big white ball as far as either of them. I practiced for three solid days after school and threw with my brothers at home; on Field Day I heaved the ball far enough to be in good standing with the President's Council, but my arm was sore for a week.

My other weakness was in basketball shooting. Carl, who was tall and had a hoop in his backyard, helped me win an Honorable Mention. But, of course, the events I really loved were in track and field. I got two first-place and two second-place ribbons in 1968, winning the 300- and the 30-yard dash and coming in second in the standing broad jump and the distance run.

The boys in my class were just beginning to act like Superior Males. They had been needling the girls for weeks about how we would lose on Field Day because of our weak female bodies. I remember the looks on their faces as I competed with them on their turf. One made the classic comment that boys seem to hand down from one generation to another. "Hey," he said, "you run pretty good . . . for a girl."

I didn't have to say anything to that. I had run on the same track with the boys and beaten most of them. I wasn't the only one, either. Di Wood cleaned a few male clocks that day in the throwing competitions. We linked arms and felt invincible.

Fifth grade was the year of the timeline. We started with timelines of our personal lives and moved on to deal with what had happened in the world in our lifetimes. The years between 1957 and 1968 were full of significant historical events. We plotted the Kennedy assassinations, the Voting Rights Act, the fires in Detroit, and the Tet Offensive, all in neat, equal dots on our timelines. I recorded what was to me a momentous event—the day the great skier Billy Kidd broke his leg. Perhaps I had a premonition.

I think those exercises clued us in to the weight of the times in which we lived. It seemed as if everyone of great importance to the world was dying off: Khrushchev, Nasser, Nehru, King, Kennedy—the list kept growing longer as we watched the news on television. If you saw the words "Special Bulletin" on the screen, you knew that someone the world needed for its balance was dead. It may be that every ten-year span is as full of disaster as that one was, and my awareness may have been heightened by inexperience. But, had it not been for a classmate who doggedly plotted the career of "Al Loucinder" at UCLA, I might have become too solemn when I perused the display of timelines. It looked as though history might crush us all. But Reita Andren and Janet Hill, our fifth-grade teachers, fought that attitude. They read inspirational books about people who beat the odds: the one I remember best detailed the adventures of a boy lost on Maine's Mount Katahdin. He overcame outrageously high odds to persevere in the wilderness. In the first few days he was scratched bloody by thorns, half starved, and nearly frozen in a weather change. He learned to feed himself and keep warm; he never lost hope. Eventually he walked off the mountain and was found.

By such means, Mrs. Andren and Mrs. Hill said, in effect, "You think one person can't do anything? Here's what one person can do."

Reita and our other teachers didn't make Cottage Farms what it was, or at least not entirely. My father had attended the school long before and his memories are as pleasant as mine. The atmosphere of that little schoolhouse, with its creaky wooden flooors and big, sun-catching windows, was such that you felt secure, able to get on with whatever you had to do. Neither changes in teachers and students nor the times disturbed the serenity. We weren't put to the torture of learning the Palmer method and our pigtails weren't dipped in the inkwells, but we sat at the same desks our parents had used and looked upon our teachers with the same amount of respect. I suppose Cottage Farms was an anachronism, upholding the things that had been good enough for our parents and were good enough for us.

I only wish I could send my children to Cottage Farms. I learned to love track and field there; I first saw how limitless the possibilities for my life were while I grumbled under Reita Andren's discipline; in the end I took over part of that discipline, which was what my teachers and parents had in mind. It would be comforting to think that other schools will do as good a job for my children, but I wonder. Cottage Farms was small enough to make individual attention possible. I sense there is less and less of that in our country's schools, what with consolidation because of tax considerations.

Unlike the gymkana, which provided merely technical information about running, Cottage Farms had a lasting effect on my career. Somebody has to help an athlete learn discipline and perseverance: my teachers helped. Somebody had to encourage me to find all sorts of interests so that when I grew up I could say, "Yes, I run, but I'm not just a runner." My teachers, along with my parents, opened the world up to me. Somebody had to give me enough sense of myself and of security about my place in the universe to enable me to go out and compete without losing my moorings. Cottage Farms taught me that I could carry my home with me because my home *was* me; it was a series of lessons and memories I could always find inside.

There is no advice I can offer to young athletes that is more important than this: if you are lucky enough to spend your childhood in such a place, surrounded by people who care about you and want you to be happy, do it. Maybe your climb to the top of your sport will be more difficult if you can't attend an academy for twenty-four-hour coaching; but then again, if you do fall there will be something underneath to catch you. When you look around to see who's manning the safety net, it will be you. A neat trick, and one I recommend.

THREE

I was beginning to grow serious about tennis, and Cape Elizabeth operated a summer recreation program where we could play competitive tennis and softball. The coaches were teachers from the high school, Sue and Keith Weatherbie among them. I played tennis for Sue and also at the Portland Country Club in its summer program. In both Cape Elizabeth and club tournaments, Anne Peabody and I were winners.

So I was feeling good about my athletic abilities by the end of the summer of 1968, and when Di Wood suggested that we go off to camp together in August, I thought that would be fun—we would be outside most of the time, running around, learning useful skills like archery and horsemanship. My parents agreed to send me for two weeks of the camp's final term.

At the beginning I was very homesick. Di and I felt like pariahs from our arrival at camp; we were new, and the other campers let us know what our limitations were. Di and I were assigned the same cabin, but our schedules had us going in opposite directions. When I failed a swimming test because I couldn't float, I was ready to pack my bags and go home. My swimming was fine; it was gravity that was against me. Nobody had told me that I'd lose half my buoyancy when I switched from saltwater to freshwater.

This was my first time away from home alone; it was natural to be homesick. Still, the other campers made it worse by continuing to ignore me. I wasn't let in on any of the private jokes that swirled around our cabin, so of course I thought most of them concerned me. I tried to sleep with my head under my pillow so I wouldn't hear them whispering and giggling. Little girls in big groups can be devastating.

Di wasn't getting along any better. I'm not usually consoled by the bad fortune of others; but I suppose I figured that if fun, outgoing Di was in bad shape and I was in bad shape, it couldn't be our fault. We exchanged grim looks and complained to each other as often as possible.

Suddenly, near the end of our term, things changed. "Today is College Day," I wrote to my mother. "It's when you have all these events."

There were sports I wasn't good at—swimming, archery, riding, and gymnastics—so I was not one of the first people picked by the captain of my Springfield team. But because I could run, I made a big contribution to the team. Springfield wiped up the track, even though Di was competing against us.

All at once, girls who had taken pains not to look at me put their arms around me and squealed their congratulations. I extricated myself from dozens of enthusiastic hugs that day. I looked at the huggers and wondered about the source of all this affection. I had similar feelings eleven years later, after I won my first Boston Marathon; I suddenly gained many "old" friends I didn't recognize.

The adulation was more embarrassing than gratifying. In

any case, it came too late to redeem the camp. I had wanted to be liked and accepted for the person I was, not because I could run and jump well. It was fun to show them what I could do, though. The instant fame present at that evening's campfire made me nervous, but my eyes misted over with the sentiment of it all—the toasted marshmallows, the singing of camp songs, the hand-holding and reminiscing.

I can't blame my bad experience on my failure to pass the water test, but it was a terrible beginning. It also served to remind me of my ongoing problem with swimming, one that had started two summers before.

Our neighborhood had a right-of-way that led to a small beach. The beach was a two-minute walk from our house, so I spent a lot of time there in summer. The neighborhood beach association hired a lifeguard for the summer, so children over eight years old were allowed to swim there unaccompanied by their parents. The lifeguard was an exceptional swimmer and he liked kids who could swim. He was also a Red Cross certified instructor in water safety; every summer he gave out certificates to kids who passed the Red Cross swimming tests.

While I did not sink like a piece of lead in saltwater, I was no great swimmer either. Every summer I was determined to show that lifeguard I could pass his tests, and every summer I failed. No matter how hard I tried I couldn't learn how to swim underwater for any reasonable distance. Every year the lifeguard watched me try once, then as much as said I should forget it. I think he believed I was hopeless.

But I refused to be discouraged. I was angry when he didn't see—or at least didn't acknowledge—the work I was putting in when I could have been goofing around with my friends. His attitude made me so mad I vowed I would never give up.

I kept working at it for the next three summers and at the Boys' Club during the winters. (They were draconian in the matter of learning to tread water at the Boys' Club; I was sure they'd let me drown if I didn't tread like mad.) Finally, when I was thirteen, I earned my Junior Lifesaving and Water Safety card. I made sure to earn it at the beach, just as all my friends had years before. Somehow, that made us all equal. More important, though, it showed the lifeguard a thing or two.

It wasn't vindictiveness that drove me to do such things, and that's not the emotion that prompts me to write about them now. My feelings were hurt, not so much by the lifeguard as by my own limitations. I looked up to him because he was one of the best athletes my town had produced; I wanted to impress him and never did. He had no idea I was knocking myself out for a few kind words. When he gave me my card he didn't throw it at my feet in the wet sand and say "Aha!" or anything. It wasn't his fault that he loved swimmers to distraction; swimming was his passion and he had no time for timid "minnows" who couldn't swim a few lousy yards underwater. It was important for me to show him I was a good swimmer, not that he had been wrong. That was what made earning the card—with his signature at the bottom—so sweet.

It was a long time before I was comfortable trying to swim. Swimming was "the" sport in high school; our town had just built a new high school and installed a pool (an almost unheard-of luxury in Maine at that time), and most of us felt we should justify the cost by using it. I wanted in the worst way to be on the swimming team, but I wasn't good enough. Until you have been to a succession of parties at which everyone else smells of chlorine, you will not understand why not being good enough was such a painful thing.

I must have learned a lesson from hovering on the outside of that elite group; I didn't appreciate it at the time, however. I knew I didn't deserve to have everything I desired, but my heart said, "Okay, but why can't I have this one thing?"

My heart continued to bug me about swimming until I put an end to the longing at Bowdoin College. During my freshman year, when the only sports I cared about were field hockey and running, I dragged myself to the pool as often as possible and taught myself to swim. Period. The coach of the Cape Elizabeth team wasn't there to pat me on the back, and nobody at Bowdoin cared whether I swam or not, but I had to learn. I showed myself that sometimes you can get what you want if you are willing to do it without looking for glory.

Swimming has become a vital part of my life, so those hours in the Bowdoin pool were well spent. Because I have suffered injuries requiring surgery on my knee and heels, there have been long periods of time when I've been unable to run as much as I would like. A stationary bicycle helps keep my legs and lungs in condition, but swimming is the best all-around exercise for me. It drains me the way running does. If I don't use a certain amount of energy in exercise every day I become almost disoriented: I can't think clearly, I'm grumpy, and I can't sit still. Swimming a mile, followed by a half hour of running in the water with the aid of a buoyant vest, sets me up for the day.

Scott Samuelson and I had been married for over a year when he turned to me one day and said, "You really are an athlete!"

I was recuperating from heel surgery at the time. Every morning I rose at six thirty, drove to a local pool, swam a mile, and came home. I lifted weights each day at a health club, and I spent forty-five minutes to an hour pumping away on the stationary bike.

Scott was accustomed to seeing me leave the house twice a day for a loop, and he'd always respected my running; but until he saw how hard I had to work to recover from an injury he hadn't thought of me as an athlete. Now he saw: this was my job, just as going to business-school classes and studying was his. What really convinced him was the swimming. He knows how much I hate to swim. I have to compel myself to use that skill—all in a day's work for an injured athlete.

Not long ago I had a letter from another marathoner who was going through her first experience with injury. She was upset, not only because she wondered about the effect of the injury on her future, but because she couldn't find a comparable exercise to do while she healed. She wanted to know how I kept myself sane when I couldn't run, but she'd never learned to swim. That made me feel grateful to the Cape Elizabeth swim team and to the lifeguard for making me mad so long before. If I hadn't forced myself to swim, I don't think I would have been able to bounce back from my many injuries. More mental than physical strength is called for in a comeback: you have to go on with a daily schedule of rigorous activity, almost pretending that nothing has set you back. The energy I released through swimming left room for my mind to function. I cannot imagine what I would have done without it.

I was asked to write this book because I am an athlete, so most of the memories I record here will relate to my athletic experiences. One point I have always been careful to make, however, is that there has never been a time in my life when

I didn't consider my development as a person to be as important as my budding career. Other things have always been going on in my life.

In June 1968 we left Cottage Farms; in September we joined the rest of the town's sixth graders and attended school at the Town Hall. Cape Elizabeth was in the throes of a population boom; neither elementary school had room for sixth-grade classes. I don't think the town officials were thrilled to have us with them day in and day out, but putting us at the Town Hall was a good temporary solution. When the high school was built the pressure was off, and the sixth grade moved to the newly formed middle school.

My teacher was strict and formal; I liked her. She upheld the standards of Cottage Farms, so there was no problem in getting on her good side: all I had to do was be myself. Since she was also the school's principal, her students took science, reading, and music from other teachers to give her time for administrative work.

My reading teacher was a rabble-rouser. He had us reading civil rights literature, antiwar statements, and stories about angry young people in the Third World. His strident opinions didn't always fly well at home. The thought that it was possible to argue with him didn't occur to me until I took his ideas home. At school, his energy was irresistible; he was always right. At home, when I translated his words into mine and presented them to my parents, most of the force was gone. My parents calmly said no, they didn't think college students should burn down buildings, and would I pass the salt? I had ideals, but I didn't know whom they belonged to; until I was sure, I stopped putting myself on the line for any issue.

I was a lot more worried about dancing school than I was about student unrest, anyway. And dancing school turned out to be fun. There was something about keeping my dress smooth and shining my shoes that made me take a new look at myself. I found I wanted to be attractive to boys. It was a big surprise, and my fledgling woman's ego didn't suffer when I was frequently asked to dance.

The summer before sixth grade I played tennis, went to the beach, watched the Red Sox, and wished I could play Little League ball. In pickup games I'd proved myself able to play as well as, if not better than, any boy my age except Chuck Poliner, who was a southpaw and could switch-hit. I couldn't understand why any regulation should keep me out of the game. I wasn't satisfied with trying to beat out the other spectators for foul balls that came over the backstop (if you turned the ball in at the snack shack you got a free Popsicle; I gave the sticks to Peter for his ship model). That was fun, but I wanted to play.

I'm sure the other girls also had inklings of their approaching womanhood, but I don't think many of our male counterparts knew what was going on. Their idea of a good time was stealing someone's stocking cap and playing keepaway with it on the playground. More and more often, I found myself standing in a small group of girls that was trying to engineer some poor boy into its matchmaking clutches. The boys, thus maneuvered into acts that proved they "liked" some girl or other, responded to the girls' teasing by diving back into the male group and threatening to throw rocks at any girl who came near. The girls were frustrated by this attitude: our hormones had shot into space, leaving the boys on the ground waving handkerchiefs.

It seemed to me that almost everything I had dreamed of doing with my life had overtones of boyishness. The climate of the times encouraged revolution, but my friends and I were slow to shoulder the barricades. As far as we could see, girls were supposed to be finished with boys' games when they were eleven. They weren't supposed to dream of careers in athletics. I can still remember watching a friend playing catch with her male teacher and being envious of her, but at the same time being glad I wasn't blatantly advertising my interest in sports. None of the girls I knew would have been flattered if described as "athletic" or (God forbid) "strong." I used to look at my brothers' high school yearbooks and hope to make the "senior superlatives" section: not as Most Athletic, but as Friendliest or Most Optimistic.

My love of sports went underground. If I had known that the boys were missing any insights into their future sexuality I would have thought they were lucky. The insights I was having made me sad and uneasy. A girl who wanted to be an athlete was suspect; maybe we could aspire to be doctors and lawyers now, but we shouldn't want muscles.

I didn't let my new attitude take me away from all sports, but the ones I played were quiet, individual ones that didn't call attention to me. I didn't talk much about Jean-Claude Killy, or the Cochran sisters (great skiers from Vermont), or Billie Jean King anymore. When asked to write about people I admired, these were the people I chose. I clipped articles about them from the Portland papers and saved them in portfolios of my dreams. But in most ways I tried to join the mainstream of my schoolmates: we talked about singers, actors, and other more acceptable celebrities.

Though I was disoriented by approaching womanhood and unhappy at its implications, I think I was lucky to have gone through an early crisis of doubt without caving in. I know all children dream of great things for themselves and sometimes the dreams die for lack of something—opportunity, ability, or resources of one kind or another. Thinking that I would be considered unfeminine should have been enough to deter me from my goals, but it wasn't. I wonder what would have become of me if I had let someone convince me that it wasn't proper for a girl to be an athlete. I had to learn to do what I believed was right—and continuing to play a variety of individual sports turned out to be the best decision I could have made; it honed my skills without making me sick of one sport.

I made adjustments. I noted which of my classmates skied on the weekends and confined my ski conversation to their presence. I stopped pasting pictures of athletes on my school notebooks. When asked what I wanted to do when I grew up, I considered the source of the question. I gave most people the second answer on my list; I should have said, "I want to be a skier, but if I can't, I'll be a teacher." What I said was "I want to be a teacher." That was much better than suffering the bemused expressions of people who were thinking "This child will never be a skier." The attitude was: nothing that good ever happens. I didn't fight it.

The worst part of this practice of separating professions into those suitable for one sex or the other was that it gave me so many doubts. I, like other adolescents, wanted to conform. It's fine to look back from this distance and see I was right in sticking to my guns, but at that time I wasn't so sure. I hung on to models like the Cochrans because I couldn't imagine giving up on sports. I had to know there were women who'd survived making athletics the primary focus of their lives.

I was still concerned enough five years later to clip an article entitled "Pastor Advocates Athletics to Better Women's Role" from the Portland *Evening Express*. According to Dr. Thomas Boslooper of the Episcopal church, it was time for men to stop thinking female athletes were unfeminine. Boslooper believed both girls and boys should be encouraged to play sports because physical fitness was integral to emotional health. He said women would always be considered the "weaker sex" as long as they were kept out of sports. Though the article concluded by quoting his assertion that well-conditioned women will have "more energy to be better mothers, housewives, lovers"—proving that his ambitions for little-girl athletes were limited—I liked the spirit in which it was written. By 1973, when it appeared, I was running in earnest, not to be persuaded to do otherwise. At the back of my mind, however, there was still a tiny voice insisting that girls shouldn't be road runners. Boslooper helped silence it forever.

So, if my athletics took a more private place in my life in the sixth grade, they also became firmly entrenched as part of my personality. I made a conscious choice in their favor. Against all good advice I still played sports: I supposed that meant I was an athlete for good or ill. I put away my baseball glove with a pang—the realization that I wasn't going to grow up to be just like Carl Yastrzemski was tough to accept, but even I had to admit that some things might never change. In the shift I picked up more tenacity for those sports I *could* play, knowing I would be allowed to participate to the limits of my ability.

The limits of my ability: these were the delineations I had begun to explore. I couldn't let anyone take the adventure away.

FOUR

The highlight of my two years in junior high school was getting the key to my own locker. This was the big time—it announced the approach of adolescence; I was deemed old enough for possessions that needed to be locked up.

The same day we received our locker keys we got a long set of rules and a privilege card. We weren't allowed to go anywhere without the yellow card; teachers signed us in and out of class and we were punished if we were caught in the halls without permission. The principal took our cards away if we broke too many rules, which meant that we had no chance to use the bathrooms or drinking fountains except in the two minutes between classes.

On one hand, they admitted that we were growing up; but on the other hand, they regulated everything we did. It was a frustrating time for all concerned. The teachers weren't thrilled to be disciplining us all the time instead of teaching, and we chafed under the routine.

There were similar problems at home. I thought my parents were too strict and old-fashioned. They were still telling me when to go to bed, what to wear, and how long to talk on the phone. I wanted them to see that I was becoming a young woman and could make some decisions for myself. When I defied them they were more determined than ever to uphold their rules.

We had some good moments when I just decided to be honest with them. One day some older kids made fun of my white ankle socks on the bus; I was still wearing my oxford shoes in the seventh grade. They pointed at me and called me names while I tried not to cry. When I got home I told my mother I wouldn't be wearing white socks anymore. She agreed that I was probably too old for them and that was that. On another occasion I asked for permission to begin shaving my legs; Mom showed me how. I was grateful to her, but at times like those I wished I had an older sister to go to for advice and comfort. My brothers were great, but I couldn't ask them to teach me womanly things. Once in a while Mom had to step away from her post as an authority figure and act like a sister, difficult as it was for both of us. I was embarrassed about putting her in that role, even to teach me to shave my legs, so I usually turned to friends for help. But I always envied my friends who had sisters.

I learned to live within my parents' boundaries because they were willing to listen to reason. They almost never changed their minds, but they were open to calm appeals and they could surprise me with leniency at the oddest times. School was different—nobody cared what I thought of the rules there.

As an adult I can understand my junior high school teachers, but it was hard to be their student. The building was overcrowded—we were still waiting for the new high school to open—and dark, old, and depressing. We didn't have any extracurricular activities to enjoy after school, so we all came and went at the same hours. We did everything together, day after day, like a herd of antelopes moving on the veld. We were a jumpy, bored mob—it was no wonder that they needed so many rules to keep us in line.

Going into the high school was like leaving a minimum security prison for the outside world. Suddenly we had choices to make, nobody was telling us where to be and what to do all the time. The Cape Elizabeth schools were led by superintendent Harold Raynolds, Jr. (now Commissioner of Education in Massachusetts), who felt that we should be given more control of our time in school. The high school offered a series of nine- and eighteen-week mini-courses in English and Social Studies from which we could pick and choose, while the other departments held on to their traditional curricula. In free periods we could elect to swim, study in the library, sit out on a sunny hillside, eat, or do anything else that didn't involve leaving campus, disturbing classes, or breaking rules.

People told Mr. Raynolds he was wrong. They said high school kids would tear the building apart unless they were kept under the strictest discipline. Here the town had spent a fortune to build a new school and he was going to let it be destroyed.

But they underestimated us. We were grateful for the building and for the freedom to experiment with it. We understood that Mr. Raynolds was depending on us to behave like responsible people. In the four years I spent at that school, I heard of only one act of vandalism: somebody set fire to a wastebasket in the boys' bathroom.

It was difficult to search out the basics in the humanities curriculum and I had to scramble to make up for holes in that foundation when I got to college. Perhaps we needed a bit more structure and less choice. But I recently heard a former teacher refer to those days as "the time of select-an-education:

one from column A, one from column B." It wasn't like that. It was the early 1970s and freedom was called for. The Raynolds system worked for me, as it did for most of the kids I knew. After two years of junior high, slumbering in the knowledge that someone else was making every decision, this was a welcome awakening.

The choices weren't confined to academic pursuits. At last I had a chance to participate in after-school activities. I told Mom I was trying out for field hockey. She was thrilled: field hockey had been her favorite sport in high school. I was worried because I'd never played before, but Mom assured me I could pick up the basics in a hurry.

Tryouts began the first week of school. The coaches, Paula Smith and Andrea Cayer, put us through hard workouts for several days; I made the junior varsity squad and occasionally played varsity. I played the center and right inner forward positions: my job was to get the ball and tear down the field with it toward the opposite team's goal.

Field hockey was the only sport open to girls in the fall; it was no easy thing to gain a spot on the team. For me it was like belonging to a popular club, and it made the transition to high school much easier. There is a camaraderie in sports, even among athletes who compete against one another, that I haven't encountered anywhere else.

Sometimes I like to be around other marathoners just because they are the only people who really understand what I do. People call me a natural athlete—and in some respects I suppose I am—but to say that is to dismiss a world of effort. Other runners know how hard I've had to train; their respect is always the sweetest to earn. Field hockey gave me my first bout with the "natural athlete" label.

I wasn't a natural hockey player. I had the speed and toughness needed, but I wasn't coordinated enough to han-

dle the stick exceptionally well. In playing the forward positions, it is important to make good passes and score when
the occasion arises. I practiced extra hours, laboring to learn
stickwork. To keep my place on the team in the meantime,
I showed the coaches I could run and use my head. They
gave me the leeway I needed, and eventually I improved my
ball-handling talents to the point where I could be counted
on for a goal almost every game. It took the same kind of
patience running takes.

The trick was never to get complacent. I liked praise as
much as anyone else, and I was praised a great deal on the
hockey field. But I knew I was capable of more—that kept
me honest. I would squirm under compliments most of the
time, not in false modesty, but because I had a voice inside
that said, "Watch it." The voice kept me ever aware of the
fact that I wasn't reaching my potential. Just because people
thought I was a good hockey player didn't mean I *was;* only
I knew whether I was giving a hundred percent. When I
played as hard and as well as my body told me I could, I
would be pleased.

Athletes understand things like that. I've been asked why
I didn't quit running marathons after the Olympics, and it's
hard to explain. But to an athlete, I can say, "Look, I haven't
given it everything I've got yet," and the other head nods.
Understood. The girls on the hockey team were equally tuned
in: they let me be unhappy about a so-so performance without reminding me that some people would be delighted with
it. They knew I was my own best motivator.

I did latch on to other sources of inspiration, though. Oddly
enough, the coaches of the opposing teams often spurred me.
Field hockey was taken very seriously in our league, so a
number of good coaches were involved. The better they were,
the more I tried to play well when we met their teams. I

always wanted to do my best around the people who loved
hockey. It was my way of demonstrating respect for their
accomplishments as coaches and former players.

Because of this penchant, I may have played my best
hockey at the Merestead Hockey and Lacrosse Camp during
the summers of 1972 and 1974. Some of the staff members
had been on British and United States national teams, some
were college coaches, and all had long backgrounds in the
sport. We played all day every day for a week. I was usually
exhausted in the late afternoon, but since we had a free hour
between our last practice and dinner I tried to run a couple
of miles a day. By the summer of 1974 I was in a running
routine that was hard to break, but I was so active on the field
that my evening outing was usually a faint trot. Still, I enjoyed pushing myself to do it.

Most of our evenings were devoted to hockey. As long as
we could see, we played, and our instructors mixed in with
us. There were no drills and very few whistles then; we were
allowed to play vigorously. I knew I was getting the best
competition I was ever likely to have, so I tried especially
hard.

I loved playing for Andrea Cayer. She was different from
any coach I'd had before and I treated her differently. I
didn't have a burning desire to show her what I could do, for
one thing. Her whole attitude said she thought we were
terrific kids who could do whatever we set our minds to. She
was no more skeptical of my talent than she was of the
ground under her feet: she supposed the talent was there and
wasn't planning to change her mind unless I proved her
wrong. Her confidence gave me confidence. I liked keeping
track of myself, by myself. Andrea knew how to admonish
or encourage me when it was appropriate, but she showed
me that I was growing up and didn't need the supervision of

Coach Legree. I've never wanted much coaching since then.

The team itself was an inspiration; everyone worked. While the local sports writers hadn't yet begun to give any girls' sport except swimming much attention, they did a decent job with hockey—we could always find some mention of our games after the golf scores from Florida.

I liked belonging to the team as much as I'd known I would back in the dark days of junior high. The satisfaction of striding around school wearing the team jacket, of having teachers I respected comment on well-played games, and of being part of a friendly, supportive group was immense. The actual playing was what I liked best, but the attendant friendships and the glory of being on a winning team didn't hurt.

Nor did the fact that I received the Most Valuable Player award after my junior season. The MVP was usually a senior, so even while I was luxuriating in success I was feeling guilty about robbing someone who wouldn't get another chance at the award. Worse, I was the track MVP freshman year. While I stood at the podium and listened to Paula Smith, the track coach, say nice things about me, I wished I could share the awards with my teammates. Their efforts helped me shine, especially in a team sport like field hockey. I wanted to say that I would have been mauled on the field without them, that we'd all worked hard for the same goals, and that nobody deserved to take so much credit. But in those days I didn't have the words. Besides, there were few speeches at the athletic association banquet. You heard your name, your face turned red, and you walked up to accept the trophy.

Maybe I deserved to be MVP in track, if you accept the idea that running is a solitary sport in which the glory belongs to the individual. I didn't think so at age fifteen and I don't now. I knew I wouldn't be as good as I was without competition from my teammates. I might have worked harder than the others because running was so agreeable to me, but they were the standards by which I measured myself. Even today I can't take full credit for a good race. I have to leave my home in Freeport a couple of times a month to find running competition; I drive to Boston and run on the track with athletes who will give me a workout. If it wasn't for their pushing I wouldn't be the same runner. I do most of my training alone, but I can't practice in a vacuum; and I certainly can't compete in one.

I'm grateful to have made this discovery so early in my career. When the high school team went to a meet, I wanted to do well for the team, not for myself.

Granted, stardom for a woman in track wasn't really imaginable in those days. If I had been thinking ahead to a lucrative career in sports I would have stuck to tennis. Chris Evert, Billie Jean King, and others were getting some deserved respect for women's tennis. But nobody was making a living by running.

Of course I was aware of my athletic talent, but it seemed to me that if I allowed myself to think I was as good as people said, I would have a long way to fall. That's why the prizes, honors, and attention don't affect me now. I'm always pleased and touched—who could help being thrilled about the Sullivan and Jesse Owens awards?—but I can't let myself believe I deserve such things. I'll lose my edge if I do that. If I start running for the awards, my career is over. I'm still running because I have a goal to reach, a time that has eluded me up to now.

In high school as now, I was motivated by success. My freshman year was so successful I couldn't believe it. The winning ways of the field hockey team sustained me even after the season was over, which was a good thing—I had less joyful experiences with the basketball team. I tried out for basketball because so many of my friends were on the team, and because it would fill a void during the weekdays when I wasn't skiing. I played on the junior varsity squad for the next three winters and never gained the coach's confidence. As soon as things got tight, I came out of the game. In my senior year I auditioned for the school play instead and loved doing it.

Throughout the winter of my freshman year I looked forward to track season, all the more so because Peter had given me a pair of running shoes for Christmas. I had wanted them for a long time, but Mom and Dad never gave me any running-related gear because they didn't want to push me into sports. These weren't my first specialty shoes—I'd bought a pair for tennis the summer before—but they were special. For years I had watched Andy and Peter compete on their high school team in Chuck Taylor shoes by Converse; people would laugh at them today. They had curled toes and looked professional. When I was twelve I took my best pair of sneakers and put them in a vise, trying to bend the toes. I had to wait two years for a pair of bona fide running shoes, but they were worth it.

They worked as advertised, too. I ran well enough to attract attention from the newspapers that spring. I tried to do everything, from running the 100, 200, and relay to the long jump. The good races are a blur in my memory, though: what I remember best is a bad experience with a coach.

I dove for the finish line while running the 100-yard dash in a meet against a western Maine school. I was brushing the dirt off my knees when the other team's coach walked over and said, "Cape may be famous for its swim team, but you don't dive on the track." She made it sound as if I had done something terribly wrong, almost illegal. I'd beaten the best sprinter in the Triple C conference, so the coach came after me out of frustration; I didn't know that at the time. She made me feel awful.

Incidents like that taught me not to crumble under adversity. If that coach meant to make me cry, she succeeded; but if she meant to break my concentration, she failed. I was all the more intent on winning after her comment—I wanted to show her I could win without diving. When her sprinter and I squared off in the 200, I won standing straight.

I can take a bad situation and make it work to my advantage: that's part of what mental toughness means. I don't know where it comes from, but it's the one attribute I know I can count on to get me through the bad times. Maybe it's a cumulative thing: the more adversity you have to face, the tougher you get (provided you meet and beat it). My body may fail me, but my head never has. There's a switch I can throw that puts me into high concentration: I focus one hundred percent on the immediate goal; I forget I have a body; I don't feel pain. It's a gift that took some nurturing. I had to use people like that coach for my own purposes. The day I refused to let her neutralize me, I took a step toward recovering from knee surgery in time to win an Olympic gold medal.

I've seen many people beat themselves. Talented people, blessed with health, education, and the love of their families, somehow find cause to give up. I know I don't have a right to judge them, because there are so many varieties of pain I haven't experienced. But I wish they could see what I have in my travels. I've watched paraplegics pushing themselves to do laps in swimming pools. Their circulation isn't good, so they feel the dead cold of the early-morning pool keenly; yet they stop after their workouts to tell me what an inspiration

I've been. (And that reminds me of an aphorism Elie Wiesel attributes to Rebbe Pinhas of Koretz: "If someone finds it necessary to honor me, that means he is more humble than I. Which means he is better and saintlier than I. Which means that I should honor him. But then, why is he honoring me?") Every time I feel sorry for myself I think of them: I rarely see a disabled person who feels helpless; robbed of some physical function, they work all the harder to develop other strengths. It's been my experience that the so-called healthy people give up first. Maybe they expect too much. People with physical limitations have lost some illusions, I suppose; they know they can't control every aspect of their lives. The rest of us expect to live forever, and when circumstances begin to wise us up, we either panic or face things straight on. The ones who panic become quitters; the ones who clench their teeth usually succeed in attaining their goals. But we all need teachers to lead us in the right direction: I learned to let adversity teach me when I was young; and now, when I'm distracted by my petty problems, I think of people whose withered bodies give them every right to complain, but who don't.

There are gentler forms of adversity, of course. A lot of my success comes down to the fact that I had to run on a substandard track throughout my high school career. A cinder track, falling apart under laughable maintenance, its major function seemed to be to contain the baseball field. Every year the field grew in a bit farther, so nobody really knew how far we were running in the name of a 440 or 880. By my senior year we must have been way outside of official range in our track events.

All in all, my freshman year was great. When it was over I basked in the summertime, took driver education classes, baby-sat, and played tennis. In August I began looking for-

ward to returning to school and field hockey. I didn't know
how important that autumn would be to my development as
a runner.

We were conference Class B champions in field hockey in
1972. Although I was absorbed in field hockey, I was also
trying other things. I was running on weekends, four or five
miles a day on Saturdays and Sundays, and as much as I
could manage during the week. Even if I only had time to do
some extra laps after practice, I did them. I almost enjoyed
fouling up in a scrimmage, because running laps was the
punishment. I liked pushing myself to keep going after exhaustion set in; it was a game I played.

My autumn running was solitary until one afternoon in
1972. I was putting my cleats on for hockey practice when
one of the boys from the cross-country team called my name.
I was late already—I'm always late—so I probably sounded
annoyed when I asked him what he wanted. He had a habit
of saying in five paragraphs what anyone else could say in
one. This time he kept it short.

"Bonny Eagle is bringing a girl to our meet this afternoon.
You want to run?"

Bonny Eagle is the high school in Buxton, west of Portland. I'd heard about the girl. As far as I knew, she was the
only girl running cross-country in the league. She trained
with the boys and roamed from meet to meet, looking for
competition. The boys on our team knew I was interested in
running, and it didn't take much to get the coaches, Paul
Jackson and Keith Weatherbie, to agree to give me a chance—
they were all for it.

I hustled out to ask Andrea Cayer's permission to run.
Mom brought my track shoes to school. While I waited for

her to arrive and for the meet to begin, I went to field hockey practice.

Five minutes before the race began I changed from cleats to shoes and presented myself at the track. I didn't think I would beat the Bonny Eagle girl, but I thought it would be fun to try. The course was only 2.5 miles: I probably ran two or three times that in every hockey practice.

As it turned out, I won easily. I ran loose and felt terrific. Little more than winded at the end of the race, I went back to hockey practice and ran laps with the team.

It was then that I got my first real inkling of my potential. I'd been training hard in hockey and running the roads, but I wasn't under anything like a tough runner's regimen, and yet I had beaten someone who was.

Victory brings odd rewards. I look at victories as milestones on a very long highway. Once clued in to my ability, I had to push myself to run better. I couldn't let it go until I had tested some of the limits. I decided to aim for the State meet in May.

The previous year's meet had been open to anyone who achieved a fairly easy standard. Almost anyone who wanted to try her luck was welcome. Girls' track was gaining in popularity, but organization lagged behind interest until my sophomore year, when official regional qualifying meets were held to determine who would go to the States.

Still, it was something to be there, if only to see how many girls in Maine were serious about running. The best team by far was from Mount Desert Island High School: they would be a major power in state running for years to come.

My giddy progress was interrupted on Pleasant Mountain that February. I went from peak-of-form to incapacity in seconds. I knew I should have felt lucky to have been in such great shape—the doctors said I would recover more quickly because of it—but mostly I was angry because I was missing so much.

Some people have written that I would never have become a runner if I hadn't broken the leg; but I had made plans to run before that. On the other hand, it is fair to say that I probably would have given my best effort to skiing had I been up to it. The leg would mend, but the part of me that didn't hold anything back when I was on the slopes was permanently damaged. I had lost my nerve. Without it, I'd never be a great skier. However, I wasn't to make this discovery until the following winter, when I tried to get back into ski racing and felt the fear. In the meantime, I stewed about my inactivity and waited for the leg to mend.

Against the vehement wishes of my parents and doctor, I was determined to run track that season. The doctor gave me a note excusing me from phys ed classes through the end of the school year; I tossed it into a wastebasket. While I was still lame I went to track practice to watch—because Mrs. Cayer wouldn't let me participate—but I ran on my own. After the little boy told me I shouldn't run while limping, I ran on the private, potholed roads of the abandoned army post near my house, hauling along until the leg stopped me. I ran every day whether I felt up to it or not. My parents must have thought I was crazy. I came home tired, nearly sick, hardly able to get upstairs to the shower. I know they wanted to stop me, but I never did stop.

It was the desire to run in the State meet that drove me. I couldn't do the sprints anymore. Even the 440 put too much strain on my leg—so I trained for the 880, which didn't require as demanding a pace as the 440. The mile was beyond me; my leg wouldn't last that distance. But the 880 was a good combination, requiring less speed than the 440 and not as much stamina. I had lost speed and stamina, so I counted on my painful hours of solo practice to build up my endurance. I settled into the 880 and came to like it.

But the highlight of the 1972 State meet was a flash of inspiration named Brook Merrow, who ran for Kennebunk High School. I watched her run the mile and was in awe of her. Her win was almost incidental to her performance—it was the way she ran that got to me. She had this determined look on her face, as if she knew she was going to blow everybody away before she started. The gritty expression never changed until she crossed the line: then she walked away and became Brook, the girl everybody liked, the one with myriad interests and a pleasant word for everyone. I fantasized about having Brook as the sister I'd always wanted: she seemed the perfect role model. I guessed she must be finding her motivation inside herself, which made me all the more determined to keep on with my self-designed running program. Brook had to find motivation inside—she had no competition on the track. Watching her, I'd finally seen the type of excellence I wanted to strive for.

I found Andrea Cayer while the stars were still floating around in front of my eyes.

"I want to run the mile," I said.

"That's because it's a glory event and you want the glory," Andrea said, kidding me.

I laughed, but knew I would have to run the mile extraordinarily well if I wanted to prove that I was in it for the love of the distance rather than for glory. Andrea's words gave me reason to push toward another goal. Now I not only wanted to run the mile, I wanted to run it faster than any girl in the state.

That summer I joined Country Runners, a club based in Buckfield and coached by Ron Thompson. We participated in cross-country races all over the state during the summer and the following year; we went wherever there were clubs to compete against. Mount Desert Island had a team, the Striders, and we saw them regularly; there were also dedicated clubs from Lewiston and Old Town. Good coaches founded teams in many areas of our state.

Two sisters from Buckfield, Joan and Karen Goodberlet, were on the team. I was lucky to be able to compete with them so often, because they were among Maine's top runners. Each took first place for her age group at the Amateur Athletic Union women's cross-country meet in Scarborough that year. The three of us went to the regionals in Amherst, Massachusetts, in November; out of a field of seventy, Karen came in twelfth and I was seventeenth.

I placed second in four AAU events on the Scarborough course that autumn. Serendipity scheduled one of those races on a day when we were playing an annual field hockey game against an out-of-state school; I went to Scarborough after the game to run. After the race I was interviewed on Portland television. The next day our athletic director told me I shouldn't be wearing my Cape field hockey jacket on TV. The jackets were part of our uniforms, he said, and not to be worn outside of school—particularly (I added silently) if we weren't participating in school-sponsored sports. That bothered me, not because I minded the lecture, but because I thought he should realize that I wore the jacket because I was proud to be on the team.

But Andrea Cayer encouraged me to run. She knew I was pounding out five miles a day and doing a lot of traveling with the Country Runners, and as long as it didn't hurt the hockey team she was all for it. She suggested I enter the annual Great Pumpkin Classic in October, and even went so far as to drive me to South Hiram for the race. There were fifty-seven runners competing; I won. Andrea exulted with me on the drive home: she talked about the need to develop such potential; all I knew was that my training was paying off and I was having a good time.

Once in a while I could get a ride from Portland to a weekend cross-country meet, and Dad would rise very early and take me to the turnpike before work. Sitting in the gray, flat light, waiting for my ride, we would chat. One day he asked me why I wanted to travel with Country Runners and add to an already busy school schedule. Didn't I want to have fun? he wondered.

I told him running *was* fun; it was a challenge and I liked challenges. He wouldn't understand it, I said, unless he did it himself. Shortly afterward he decided to give it a try—he's been running ever since. In the interim, he generally kept his bewilderment to himself.

I liked running the mile from the start that spring. I was still doing the 880 because I was fond of that, too, but I could tell that the mile was fast becoming my event.

I had already begun to compete in local road races that spring. I left Pleasant Mountain early one Saturday to run the Maine Masters 5 kilometer (3.1 miles) in Portland; it was the first time I ever left the mountain in the middle of the day. And it was worth setting the precedent—I won in a record time of twenty-one minutes flat.

The upshot of my training and competing was that I easily qualified that spring for the State 880 and the mile. I unofficially broke the 880 record (official records could be made only at the State meet) with a time of 2:24. I thought I was as ready for the States as I would ever be, but I didn't reckon on my own inexperience in track competition.

Mount Desert brought another powerhouse team to Orono. Their star miler was Joanie Westphall. I told everyone I was happy just to be in the mile—and I was—but deep down I wanted to make a good showing against Joanie.

There was the usual early jockeying for position, and soon some of the slower runners dropped back. I was trying to get by a girl in lane one when she slid over to her right; I snuck by her on the inside as she wavered between lanes. Once I was beyond her I was in the clear; I came in second, right behind Joanie.

A man came up to me as I puffed and caught my breath and said, "That's too bad."

I didn't think second place was so bad. I was happy with the results. "Anytime I can come in second when Joanie's in the race, I don't mind," I said.

"No," he said, "I mean it's too bad you were disqualified."

Apparently, there had been some contact between me and the runner in lane one. I didn't feel it, but the officials saw it and I was disqualified.

I ran the 880 and did well, but I didn't care about that. I can still remember the hurt and disappointment of that day. I had trained and trained and trained, I had run my best race, and then I was disqualified. For a minute I felt as though a whole year of my life—from the moment I'd seen Brook Merrow run the mile to that present moment—had been wasted. Then I picked myself up, mopped away the very real tears, and decided that the following year I would go for the state record. I guess I could have given up running—I was deeply hurt—but instead, I got mad. I used the hurt to my advantage in the following year; every time I wanted to quit, I remembered and kept running so that I could redeem myself at the next State meet.

I turned sixteen that spring, old enough to get a job. An intercom announcement that the guidance office was taking applications for a lighthouse keeper fired me with dreams of running through the summer on a lonely island, but when I investigated, I was told that an older woman in Portland wanted a light housekeeper. I settled for a chambermaid position at a Cape Elizabeth inn.

I ran in several AAU-sponsored road races that summer and competed outside of Maine as well. Ron Kelly, a fine runner who was helping Ron Thompson with Country Runners, took me to some meets. He invited me to go to a competition in Boston that summer; while I was there, John Babington, the coach of the Liberty Athletic Club, introduced himself.

In the fall of 1974 John invited me to join the Liberty A.C. The regional AAU was divided into three separate divisions at that time: New England encompassed Massachusetts, Rhode Island, Vermont, and New Hampshire; Maine and Connecticut were in divisions by themselves. In order to join Liberty A.C. I would have to make the switch from Maine to New England, but the club had a lot to offer. I could get transportation to bigger and better meets and might even get air fare if the club qualified for a national event. It meant a great deal to me to find stiffer competition; and since I was on a limited budget, I would have welcomed the help with transportation. But the Maine AAU didn't want to release me. I agonized over leaving them on bad terms, but in the end I did. It was the best thing for my running career, and difficult as it was, I knew I was making the correct decision. I couldn't run for Liberty right away. I had to run unattached for a year, which was not much fun. I resisted pressure from the Maine organization, even though I couldn't compete as much as I wanted to because transportation was a problem.

More and more, my running took me away from regular high school sports. I went to the Great Pumpkin Classic again in my senior year and won it in 7:45. This time I drove myself to the race—Andrea assumed that if it was important to me, I should find a way to get to races on my own. After that I ran in the National Road Runners Age Group Competition in Van Cortlandt Park in New York and finished ninth in a field of seventy-five. From there I won four AAU cross-country meets in Scarborough; my best time for 2.5 miles was 16:20. At the AAU finals in Gorham I ran 15:30 for 2.3 miles. I also scored thirteen goals in field hockey that season—it was a marvelous fall—but much as I hated to admit it, the progress I was making on the roads was overshadowing hockey.

Yet, even with the transportation problem, my running took me away. That fall, between field hockey and AAU cross-country meets and weekend road races, I qualified for the National Junior Olympic Cross-Country Championships in Raleigh, North Carolina. My parents offered to finance the trip, thinking it would be a once-in-a-lifetime chance. I certainly never thought I'd get another opportunity to go as far away as North Carolina to run.

Just thinking about flying makes me uncomfortable nowadays, but that wasn't always so. The trip to Raleigh was an adventure, my first time on a commercial airplane. I was scared about being so far from home; the plane trip kept my mind off my fright. I wasn't away for long, in any case—I flew to N.C. State on Friday, competed on Saturday, and was back in Maine on Sunday.

I made a respectable showing in the 2.5 mile race, considering that this was my first taste of national competition, but I finished far enough back in the teens to think, "Either I give this up now or I start trying harder, start really practicing." I hadn't increased my mileage beyond five miles a day. In North Carolina I realized I would have to prepare myself for cross-country if I meant to keep running the long distances.

A reporter from the Portland *Evening Express* came to school to talk to me one day in November. Her feature article made me look like a cross between Jesse Owens and Abraham Lincoln. She wrote about my good grades, my self-will, and, of course, my running. I didn't want to admit that running was important to me, even though I told the reporter, "I have to run every day. If I don't run, I feel guilty."

The problem was, I thought of running as an essentially selfish sport, while field hockey made me a team player. I wanted to be known as a generous person, one who passed the ball to the player who had the better shot at the net; I dreaded making an impression as an athletic hermit. The vows I made about running—to win the mile in the State meet, to improve as a cross-country competitor—I kept to myself. And sometimes I convinced myself that those goals weren't as worthy as the ones I set in field hockey: I even went to college thinking I might give up running for hockey.

In the moments of truth I gave my running the attention it needed to thrive, but I always felt guilty for it.

When track practice started the following spring I had a decision to make. It was my senior year and Andrea wasn't coaching the team; the new coach was a woman I didn't know. Keith Weatherbie was heading the boys' team. He'd already proven to be a great motivator, and I wanted some good coaching while I waited to join Liberty A.C. I was bound for Bowdoin College in the fall, and Bowdoin didn't have a women's running program. For all I knew, Keith would be the last influential coach I would ever have in school. So I decided to practice with the boys' team and run meets with the girls'. That didn't sit very well with the new coach, but I thought it best for my running. There was no competition on the girls' team: I had to run with the boys and be coached by Keith if I wanted to improve.

I felt way out of line all spring. I disliked putting my own interests ahead of the team's, yet I couldn't stop myself. I was even breaking school rules to run more: almost every day someone from the boys' team would sneak out of school and run with me during a free period. We weren't allowed to leave campus during the school day, but Mom was on the school board and I suppose I hoped that exempted me from some of the rules. I didn't see how anybody could object to what we were doing, but I knew it was wrong. If I spotted a police car on the road I wondered if we would be reported. We were never caught, though.

That spring I began running double workouts. I'd take the illicit run in the morning, then go to track practice in the afternoon. At the Triple C Division Championships I was first in the 880 with a time of 2:22.2, first in the 440 at 1:02.4, second in the long jump, and fifth in the 220. At the regional meet in Westbrook, where we qualified for the States, I ran the mile in 5:15, an unofficial record. I knew I had a shot at the official mark on the coming weekend.

I watched the men's finals before my race. The two-mile event turned out to be a duel between two of the best runners Maine has produced: Bruce Bickford and Jimmy Doane. Seeing them got me all pumped up; I went into my race figuring I could go at their pace for one mile if they could do it for two. I ran my first half mile at a faster pace, in fact; but then I petered out, winning in 5:29. It was a state record— and it was the fulfillment of the goal I'd held since being disqualified—but it wasn't as good as it might have been. That was a vivid lesson of the need to pace myself.

I had run better than ever before with the girls' team, but when it came time to announce the track and field MVP at the awards banquet, I didn't hear my name. I watched someone else accept the trophy. Di Wood and I shared best all-around athlete honors, but I wanted the track award. I had worked for it.

Over the summer I grew philosophical about the award.

After all, it was supposed to go to the person who contrib-uted the most to the team, and I was mostly working for myself. My path had diverged from theirs and I'd had to follow it. I tried not to forget the sting because I knew I could use it: to make my decision to run with the boys worth that awful moment, I really had to show people I could run. As they said at graduation, I had my whole life in front of me.

FIVE

I took a job that summer of 1975 at the Lobster Shack, a seafood restaurant in Cape Elizabeth. We worked in the shadow of a lighthouse, so foggy days were murder: the horn rattled our brains. I was behind the takeout counter, serving lobsters, fried clams, and french fries to hordes of tourists and locals.

I was still running unattached, so finding transportation would have been a terrible hassle if it hadn't been for Ron Kelly. He made sure I got to Boston to compete occasionally and saw to many of my needs as a runner. In October of my senior year he had taken me to a cross-country meet in Burlington, Vermont, because he knew the setup was perfect for me. Not only did Burlington High School have many fine competitors, but Johanna Forman, the top schoolgirl runner in New England, was entered. Her coach at Falmouth High School was John Carroll, now co-director of one of my favorite races, the Falmouth Road Race. Ron couldn't have known how important John Carroll's race would be in my future, but he probably realized I'd run better because John was watching. His success with Johanna impressed me and I wanted to give her a race so he would notice me. I ran as hard as I could and came in second.

Ron not only understood why I needed to compete, he understood why I loved it. As a runner himself, he'd felt the indescribable rush you get when you see your training paying off. He knew I had a great deal to learn—and often told me so—but I think he also recognized that I had more heart than I knew what to do with. That alone got me through many races before I'd learned anything about pacing myself, feeling out the other runners, and running smart. As a kid I was like someone who fixes a point on a far horizon and knows, against all rational advice from her body, that she can keep going until that point is reached. I ran flat out whenever I competed and there was always something left. I've watched fans at basketball and baseball games who stand up and scream and shake when their team wins; that's the feeling I had when I ran my hardest. It didn't have as much to do with winning as it did with making it to that point on the horizon—it's wonderful to do something when your own body has its doubts.

I ran a 5:03.8 mile in Albany, New York, and qualified for the Junior Olympic Nationals. I was closing in on a sub–five-minute mile. Like all of my best coaches and advisers, Ron knew that the way to motivate me was to tell me about other runners and what they were accomplishing. Before I reached Albany Ron fed my competitors' statistics to me. I didn't turn out to be the top runner there, but I qualified. I hoped I had the mettle to go on alone at the national level, but was grateful I didn't have to try. Ron wasn't just an inspiring athlete, he was a teacher. He helped me find the scope of my own potential.

The nationals were held at Cornell University in August. The athletes were divided by regional districts and I was one of the first to arrive from mine. I checked in to my room alone, then went to dinner. On my way back I walked slowly, enjoying a few fresh breezes after the hot day. I stopped to talk to two white-blond swimmers who were sitting on a wall swinging their legs.

"Where are you from?" one boy asked.

"Maine," I said.

They looked at each other and laughed.

"What's so funny?"

"We used to live in Maine," one said, still giggling. "But our fathers got jobs, so we moved."

California, no doubt, I thought as I walked on. I used to think you had to come from California to be a great athlete. The swimmers made me want to prove that you didn't have to leave Maine to find good coaching. The best coaching could come from within the athlete, so it didn't matter where he or she was geographically located.

That seems to be especially true for distance runners. Not that they don't need coaching—I think I am unique in my approach to training and I don't necessarily recommend that anyone else try to go it alone—but they do not need to come from California or its equivalent. Grete Waitz, Bill Rodgers, Ingrid Kristiansen, Jim Ryun—all were reared in cold climates, though many choose to do part of their training in warmer places.

I have a couple of theories about why top long-distance runners have emerged from places like New England and Norway. I think we learn to cope with physical hardship by participating in athletics in all varieties of weather. I have spots of frostbite on my fingers and toes from marathon skiing sessions, but I carry less dramatic evidence as well: memories of hiking and fishing in icy rain showers, rowing into a fierce cold wind, running meets in sudden May hail.

We learned not to expect cooperation from the weather; we didn't let it slow us down too much. My second theory involves cross training. Ingrid and I—and many other distance runners—have skiing backgrounds. Like me, she is an avid cross-country skier. Perhaps there is something complementary about cross-country skiing and running, some ideal interaction of muscles that fits the legs for marathoning. For one thing, I think cross-country skiing strengthens the arms, bringing the upper body more into sync with the normally stronger lower body of a runner. The body that is more in sync is apt to be more efficient in its operation.

You can see I've brooded about that insult to my home state. But I actually felt sorry for those two swimmers who missed growing up in Maine. I don't think they would have appreciated my sympathy. I didn't let their comments bother me in the weekend competition, in any case. I ran the mile in 5:01.1, not a winning time, but two seconds better than my previous best. The sub–five-minute mark still eluded me, but I was chipping away at it.

Freshmen were expected on the Bowdoin campus before Labor Day. I had to hurry with my preparations once I got home from Cornell.

I was sure Bowdoin was right for me. In elementary school my friends and I talked about college—most of us wanted to go to Bowdoin. This was before the college went coeducational, and I don't remember what we based our hopes on.

I weighed other options for myself during high school. At one point I was certain I would be happiest if I enrolled in Westbrook College's two-year dental hygiene program. I considered the University of Vermont because it had a superior ski team. I thought about Brown University for a time; one of my summer field hockey coaches was from Brown. But everything brought me back to the nagging belief that nothing would replace Bowdoin. Its new admissions policy, designed to attract a well-rounded student body, helped me make up my mind to apply for early decision. Bowdoin didn't require SATs. Instead, applicants could submit artwork, write music, perform a musical or dramatic audition, whatever. We had to write two essays, one on a subject of our choice and one about our hopes for our future; from there we could demonstrate individuality and worthiness in our own way. I sent clippings of my running and field hockey results and, for good measure, an essay about Emily Dickinson. When I got an acceptance letter, I felt as if the gates of heaven had just swung open.

Only one thing gave me pause: the lack of a women's running program. But I got a letter in the summer saying that another freshman, Anne Marie Goldstein from Virginia, wanted to start a cross-country team for women. However, the team didn't materialize that fall. Maybe if it had I wouldn't have been so high on the idea of playing field hockey, but I had to find time for both sports.

Even though running had become more and more important to me, I still loved hockey and felt that it was going to be my college sport. I wasn't thinking of becoming a professional athlete—as a hockey player, the furthest I might go would be to compete on the national team and coach at a college. I wanted to earn a Bowdoin degree while playing sports on the side, then get a job in my chosen profession.

Running might have taken over from hockey if I'd had a coach structuring my workouts, pushing me at it. Instead, I ran in my free time, before and after hockey practices. My studies may have suffered slightly as I adjusted my sports schedule, but, again, I think the pressure was good for me. I had another tough demonstration of just how important running was to me; I would go out and run five miles after the grueling afternoons on the field. And I may have been saved from one year too many of a single-minded devotion to a particular sport. When I was a freshman I resembled the Cottage Farms kid more than the adult I would become. I still loved to fool around with all sorts of athletic activities. If I'd given up my beloved field hockey without a real test to see whether I preferred it to running, I might have knocked over one of the supports that have kept me going as a runner.

I like to compare Joan Benoit, the athlete, to a pyramid. I started my running life with a wide foundation in sports—tennis, skiing, baseball, and all the others. Slowly, my interests narrowed. The pyramid rose and headed toward a point at the top. I haven't reached that point yet, which is why I'm still running. Other people—some of the products of the Cape Elizabeth swimming program, for instance—reversed the pyramid. They started with an obsession to swim and tried to build the infrastructure of an athletic career on top of that tiny little point. The giant complex teetered more and more frequently as they got older until it finally came crashing down on itself. No one from that program has gone on to become a world-class swimmer, though the talent seemed to be there in a couple of cases. Of course Maine isn't exactly a breeding ground for swimmers, and not everyone has the drive to stay with a sport—especially one as demanding as swimming. But these kids were beautifully coached and appeared to be dedicated. My best explanation is that they woke up one morning and began to wonder if their lives outside the pool had any meaning. Where had they been while the rest of us played pickup basketball games? Why were they chasing a dream whose origins they could no longer pinpoint? Had they really tried to build their whole lives around swimming? My theory is that they weren't swimming to please themselves. Satisfying yourself is the key to any success, but especially in athletics. You have to know, deep inside, that you love what you are doing—not because the coach or your parents want it for you, but because you desire it yourself.

As I made more room for running, I regretted some of the things I had to give up. But I made my decisions from a position of strength. I knew who I was, I knew where my dreams came from, and I knew I would never have to settle too much of my self-esteem on one achievement. As I've said before, I was lucky.

I made the varsity field hockey squad my freshman year. We had a good season and I kept my spot all the way through. I was running forty or fifty miles a week and participating in meets on the weekend, but the hockey coach, Sally LaPointe, didn't object as long as my play didn't suffer. By the next fall, however, I was so involved in running that I had to make a choice. I could run on the new women's cross-country club or play hockey. The club wasn't large and it wasn't a college-sanctioned team, but it would give me the chance to train with women. I could also train harder with the men's team if I wasn't playing hockey every day.

But I loved hockey. I asked the coach to give me a couple of days to make up my mind after practice began. I would run, then go to the field and watch practice, then run again. I knew I would miss the camaraderie of the team, but I had to run more if I was going to improve.

Finally, I decided to go out for hockey, figuring I could make time for running. It seemed like a mature choice, but it didn't work out. The coach was uncertain of my commitment from then on—I had to earn my varsity spot again and didn't play much in the first few games. But by the end of September she was starting me.

On October 1 the team went to Rhode Island to play

Brown and URI. We weren't expected to do well; we surprised everyone by tying one game and winning the other.

Sunday morning I ran in the Portland Elks Half-Marathon and placed second to Charlotte Lettis in 1:19:24. Charlotte was a legend, a pioneer in women's running; it was practically an honor to be beaten by her. But the two highlights of that race involved men: I beat my brother Andy for the first time, and I got Bill Rodgers' autograph.

I was tired that night, but made my classes the next morning. The worst part of the day came later, though, in a hockey game with Colby College in Waterville. We were supposed to win, but again, we confounded the predictions. I was so tired I couldn't move during the opening half; at halftime, the coach benched me.

I was demoted to the JV squad. I thought about quitting, but the word nearly gives me hives. Besides, even in my frustration I recognized the fairness of the coach's reaction. I hadn't lied about the Portland race, but neither had I asked her permission to run in it. She had a right to ask the varsity players to keep themselves in top condition for games; by running on Sunday I had sabotaged my own performance and let the team down. So I played JV, determined to show her I had the guts to stick with it.

Soon I was playing the best hockey of my life. I kept waiting for a reprieve, but the coach held firm. I was too accomplished for JV play; we were beating everyone on our schedule and I was bored to death. But that didn't matter to the coach. Perhaps she wanted to prove that no one was irreplaceable. I never played varsity again.

I made my last stand at a game with the University of Maine at Portland-Gorham (now the University of Southern Maine). I was mad that day and wanted to be back playing with the varsity team. I walked onto that field with a mission and played the game of my life. I was everywhere; nobody could defend against me. I kept asking my body for more, pouring reserves of energy and savvy into my game until I felt it was almost beyond my own control. Then, near the end of the second half, I stepped into a divot and twisted my knee. I watched the closing minutes of the game from the bench.

At the Bowdoin infirmary, the injury was examined by the college physician, Dan Hanley, a cousin by marriage. He all but told me that I was crazy to continue playing field hockey. A friend of his had seen me running at the Olympic trials in Oregon the previous summer and asked Dan how serious I was about running. He told the friend I hadn't spent much time with it, relatively speaking, and the friend said, "Well, she's got potential."

"This man knows what he's talking about, Joanie," Dan said. "Why in the world would you want to ruin yourself playing lateral-motion sports when your talent is for running? You should forget about hockey."

It was all I could do to keep from leaping off the table and saying "Aye, aye, sir." It helped that he was supporting my decision to end my field hockey career. Dan has long been involved with the Olympic Committee and has been an athlete: if anyone was fit to advise me, he was.

From here on I began seriously pursuing a running career. The knee injury gave me a chance to get used to the idea of never playing field hockey again. When Dan said there was no future in it he was only echoing my own thoughts. Running was the obvious choice for me. I could run for the rest of my life. After all the agony, the final decision was, ironically, easy to make. It seemed poetic, too: at least I was moving ahead, not from side to side.

. . .

Field hockey wasn't the only thing on my mind during my first two years at Bowdoin. I was busy trying to juggle sports, academics, and social activities; I never really emerged from the muddle this put me in, but I grew accustomed to it. I joined the Delta Kappa Epsilon fraternity in my first semester—women were admitted to all fraternities on campus. I made close friends there and didn't feel the isolation common in the life of an athlete.

I increased my running mileage to fifty miles a week in that first semester and did most of the work alone. But I was seriously aiming at the sub–five-minute mile, so I knew I needed to test myself by training with other runners. I was welcomed to the men's cross-country practices with enthusiasm, partly because my brother Peter was on the team, and partly because of my high school record. I ran with them on Sundays. I was glad hockey practice kept me from being with them every day because I might have held them back. They ran ten or twelve miles each day and I wondered what I was doing on the road with them, it was so hard. The men's coach, Frank Sabasteanski, who had been an Olympic coach in the weight events, was at first skeptical of my presence. Eventually I proved I wouldn't drag the team down, what with Frank standing at different spots along our training course saying "Pick up your *heels*, Benoit!"

One of my biggest races that first fall was a three-mile cross-country event in Exeter, New Hampshire, which I won in 17:40.2. Jeff Johnson, then the Exeter High School coach, awarded me a pair of red Nike waffle trainers as first prize. Those shoes were revolutionary at the time, so I felt terrific wearing them. More important, the race was the beginning of a long friendship with Jeff, who had recently helped launch Nike, Inc. He was one of the driving forces behind the company's success and did more than anyone I can think of to build up the sport of women's running. Even by the mid-seventies women weren't taken seriously as distance runners, but Jeff kept encouraging them. In 1985 he started coaching the Oyster River, New Hampshire, cross-country team. He took a bunch that hadn't won a meet in years to an undefeated regular season and third place in the state championship. Sometimes, when the uproar in my life threatens to overwhelm me, I think about Jeff. He found a way to prosper, then shared his prosperity with the kids in Oyster River. I hope I'll have that much sense when it's time to slow down.

I tried to keep my competition at a minimum during hockey season. When I returned to Bowdoin after the Christmas break I had much more leeway in my schedule. I chose to run the JV mile with the men's track team so I could proudly wear a Bowdoin singlet, but most of my running was for Liberty A.C. At last I was a member of the club. John Babington would pick me up at the Boston bus station and drive me to meets, and if I was anxious about missing too much school he would drive me all the way back to Maine so I could study comfortably in the backseat.

John probably knew I was wearing myself out. He must have realized, too, that simply telling me to organize my life more effectively wasn't enough. As long as I could keep going at a frantic pace, I would do that. I've had to face the fact that mine is an obsessive personality: sometimes my goals become more important than good sense. I keep pushing until I literally drop.

It took me a long time to bring college under control. Classes were more demanding than I'd imagined they could be, hockey at that level was real work, living with roommates—even with good friends like Kathy Graff and Karen Brodie—was a matter of making daily adjustments to one another, and running was demanding more time than ever. As a fraternity pledge, then as a brother, I was expected to devote myself to projects within the house. There was never enough time to do anything really well or completely. I was playing catch-up everywhere I went.

John obviously heard the tension in my voice when we spoke about upcoming meets. He would try to give me training advice, but that wasn't what I wanted from him. I needed him to motivate me, to get me fired up enough to find the extra hours for running. What he finally did was tell me about a high school runner named Lynn Jennings. She was setting all kinds of records for Harvard High School in Massachusetts. John has a tremendous talent for spotting potential, even when he has nothing to go on but newspaper clippings, so it wasn't surprising that he found Lynn Jennings. He invited her to join Liberty, then asked me to watch her run. He had to ask me more than once because I felt so guilty about leaving Bowdoin. When I finally saw Lynn going through her workouts I didn't know what to think. She looked great, but without running against her I couldn't gauge her talent.

Lynn and I met at a track meet in Boston in 1976. I was still recovering from the second part of John's motivational scheme: in January he'd taken me to the Dartmouth Relays, where my time for the mile was 5:10.5, a dismal nine seconds slower than my best. If that wasn't bad enough, the next day I ran the 3,000 meter in ten minutes and twelve seconds, adding twenty-one seconds to the time I'd set the previous May at the AAU Junior Nationals. Something had to give and John knew it. He arranged for me to compete against Lynn in a 1,500m race, which she won. That scared me out of my slump. I trained with a will, and in February, thanks in part to Lynn and John, I had a major breakthrough. I broke the five-minute mile at the New England AAU championship on the old University of Rhode Island wooden track (I had an edge against my competitors: after working out at Cape Elizabeth High and Bowdoin, the slow URI track, with its banked sides, held no horrors for me). I came in second to Charlotte Lettis, but the thing that mattered most was my time: 4:57.5. Shame at Dartmouth and fear in Boston prompted that terrific moment.

I still fear Lynn Jennings. She reminds me of me. She has the same mental toughness, the same ability to concentrate that has taken me through an unpredictable career. She, too, got to college and found she was spread too thin, so rather than let herself be run ragged by everyone else's expectations, she gave up competition for a while to earn a Princeton degree. The strategy worked: she set personal records all over Europe in 1985. Her best races are the 3,000, 5,000, and 10,000m; her times seem to improve with each passing month.

In 1985 Lynn knit a sweater for me to say "thanks for being there and being an inspiration." She's done it all herself, of course, and what she doesn't know is how much help she was to me when I was letting myself slide in college. I consider her to be one of the best of the new wave of runners, those who will top my records and those of Ingrid Kristiansen and Mary Slaney. That should be an inspiration to anyone trying to make a comeback: it can be done if you stay healthy and have the head for it.

I tried to regulate myself better after the URI meet so that I could stay in shape for the spring and summer seasons. I concentrated on creating an effective balance between academics and running and, for the most part, it worked. When I think back I see myself studying or running all the time. I don't remember goofing off with my friends very much, which is something I regret. My roommates constantly invited me to go to the movies or out on the town, but I usually said, "No thanks, I have to study."

On April 22 a dream came true. I went to Philadelphia for the prestigious Penn Relays. Bill Cosby talked about running in the Penn Relays on some of his records: I couldn't believe I was actually there.

The track at Franklin Field was superb, of course, because running has always been popular at Penn. I'd never seen anything like the enthusiasm—there were more spectators for this one meet than Bowdoin had for its entire football schedule.

On the first day I took fourth in the 1,500 with a time of 4:28.27. I was trying to run the 1,500 as often as possible because the Olympics were coming up and the 1,500 was the longest women's race in the Games. (The following summer I was invited to fill out the 1,500 field at the trials in Eugene. I hadn't achieved the qualifying time, but there were a few spots left for additional runners. I came in near the bottom of the pack, but at least Dan Hanley's friend saw me run and alerted him to my potential.)

Two days later I ran the anchor leg of the 1,600m relay for Liberty A.C. I got the baton two hundred meters behind the next-to-last team, so there wasn't much hope. But I gave it everything I had and then some—effort is always worth something. On the back turn I passed the section of stands where some spectators had been playing bongo drums throughout most of the meet. They pushed the already heady atmosphere of Franklin Field a notch higher. As I ran by them I heard someone yell, "Go, little honky, go!"

I still count that as one of the highlights of my career. Just for the bongo players I found some more speed and ended up running the fastest 400 of my life, a 59.8. Alas, this wasn't *Rocky*—we didn't win the race.

In May I ran my first L'eggs Mini Marathon in New York City, finishing fourth to Julie Shea of North Carolina State. The Mini was a milestone for female runners. I think some of the New York sportswriters expected the race to die a swift death because there were no men involved—it was assumed that an all-female event wasn't interesting enough to attract spectators. But L'eggs took a chance and it paid off. Now the Mini attracts running stars from all over the world; the company pays appearance fees, for which the leading runners are expected to be visible at the pre- and post-race social events and clinics, hand out the prizes, and do promotional interviews. L'eggs still maintains a policy of giving runners, young and old, an opportunity to test themselves against the big names—in 1986 there were over eight thousand entrants. Without this race and others, I wouldn't have been able to prove that I was worth backing and couldn't have afforded to continue running.

In June I went to the Junior and Senior AAU National meets at UCLA and saw Jan Merrill set a new American record in the 3,000. My seventh place was satisfactory, given the quality of the field. I really looked up to Jan. She was one of the best track runners in the country during the late 1970s and early '80s. Besides that, she was from New England. There was hope for me yet.

I've gotten to know Jan well in recent years—her aunt and uncle had a house in Freeport, where I live—and I'm very fond of her. She is funny, intelligent, and shows the maturity of someone who has handled some bad breaks. The 1980 Olympic boycott dealt her a terrible blow; she was ready to win gold medals that year.

I won the Falmouth Road Race on Cape Cod on my first

try that summer, and it was just like being in my own back-yard. Shore Road in Falmouth reminds me of Shore Road in Cape Elizabeth—there are lots of twists and turns and inter-esting views of the ocean. Through 1986 I have run in Falmouth eight times and won six. My first victory there was in 1976, when I crossed the line in 43:08; in 1985 my time was 36:17.7. Every year I think I can't possibly run the course any faster, but except for poor showings in 1980 and 1986, I always have.

Falmouth is special. The morning of the race I am taken by friends to the starting line in a boat, which I recommend to anyone who wants to put her head in order and confront an imminent task. At least one person always asks whether the motion hasn't given me sea legs. But I was born to jump from boats into footraces. Besides, I'd rather have sea legs than a monster headache—I don't have to worry about miss-ing the gun because I'm stuck in traffic en route to Woods Hole.

In 1983 I won Falmouth the day after a friend's wedding. A reporter asked what helped me to set a new course record. I said I'd run entirely on wedding cake and champagne. I wouldn't dare say such a thing in Chicago or New York: I can see the headlines about my addictions to booze and junk food. But Massachusetts writers understand me and know when I'm kidding.

I don't know why runners develop deep affinities for cer-tain races. Grete Waitz is practically the soul of the New York Marathon, for instance. As often as Grete has run New York or I've run Falmouth, these races are more like training runs for us. But there are disadvantages to knowing a course that well: the first time I ran the Boston Marathon I turned to a man running next to me and said, "So, where is this famous Heartbreak Hill?" and he said, "We just passed it."

The next time I knew when to expect the hill and wasn't quite as easygoing. But familiarity does make a race special for me, which is why I do well in the Boston races. I love to run the Tufts 10k (formerly the Bonne Bell), the Boston Marathon, and the Falmouth Road Race. Not only have these events given me huge career boosts, Bostonians have also adopted me as a hometown hero. I won't run in front of Boston people when I can't give it my best effort, because they deserve my best. They've supported me, picked me up with their cheers on any number of cold, drizzly days when they could have been inside watching the race on TV, and taken me into their hearts. I think Grete feels similarly about running in New York. When she came here in the 1970s she was unsure of her English and very shy. After achieving a world record at the New York Marathon in 1978, she was the darling of the city. She's gone on to perform exceptionally well at the L'eggs Mini Marathon, too. The fans are just as important to runners as they are to any other athletes, even if we sometimes appear not to notice them.

In the 1970s running wasn't getting the attention it enjoys today, but with large yearly increases in the number of recreational runners, it was only a matter of time before we were noticed. Women's running, especially, picked up irresistible momentum.

The January 1986 issue of *Runner's World* magazine featured an article about the history of women in running by Joan Ullyot (who ran in the first International Marathon, for women only, in Waldniel, West Germany, in 1974). The article gives the impression that there was a reservoir of female talent being held back by a dam of male resistance: when the dam broke, a flood was loosed that is still raging today, though perhaps less violently. As early as 1966, Roberta Gibb and Doris Heritage Brown were trying to gain recognition. Brown was disqualified from AAU competition for running against men (she didn't have much choice). Gibb entered the 1966 Boston Marathon as "Bobbi Gibb," but she wasn't trying to fool anyone—there was no written rule barring women from running at Boston. Many people who saw Roberta run assumed she'd jumped in somewhere in the middle, since women supposedly weren't capable of running that far.

Things moved quickly after that. In 1967 Katherine Switzer was the subject of sensational attention in Boston when Jock Semple, the marathon's director, ejected her from the course. Bobbi Gibb ran that year, too, but it was Katherine who was challenged. She inspired other women to enter races—even though they couldn't do so officially—and running clubs in several major American cities began to admit women. According to Ullyot, the San Francisco Dolphin Sound End Runners "gave equal numbers of place awards to men and women, though women made up less than 10 percent of the field."

In 1972 the AAU, faced, as Ullyot says, with a fait accompli, allowed women to compete in races of all distances. But a final barrier remained. Women were told that they would have to start any marathon ten minutes before the men. Nina Kuscsik, who may be more responsible than anyone for making women's running a visible and competitive sport, led a sit-in at the 1972 New York Marathon. She and the other female athletes refused to start when the gun sounded for them; instead, they waited for the men's race to begin and joined in. Nina ran an unofficial 3:08 that day; she added ten minutes to her official time because the cause was something she believed in. And the protest worked: the rule was never applied again.

More women joined the sport, more records were made

Top: A shirtful of blue ribbons does not excite my cousins or my brother Peter (far right).

Left: I'm ahead to stay, a mile from the finish of the Portland Boys' Club five-mile race on Patriot's Day, 1975. *(Andrea Cayer)*

Right: The finish of the 1979 Boston Marathon. *(Steven E. Sutton/Duomo)*

Top: A police escort after the 1979 Boston Marathon. *(Steven E. Sutton/Duomo)*

Above: Shaking hands with Rosalynn Carter at the White House. *(Mary Anne Fackelman/The White House)*

Mary Shea beating me in the 10,000-meter run at the 1979 AAU Nationals in Walnut Creek, California. *(Paul J. Sutton/Duomo)*

Just before the Natural Light Half-Marathon, Orleans, Massachusetts, July 1980. I won, setting a personal record for the distance.

Grete Waitz (left) winning the L'eggs Mini Marathon in New York City's Central Park in 1982, over me (second place) and Charlotte Teske. *(Sailer/McManus)*

Left: I lost the 2,000-meter Vitalis Olympic Invitational at the Meadowlands in New Jersey in 1983 to Patti Sue Plummer by one one-hundredth of a second. *(Sailer/McManus)*

Right: Hitting the tape at the 1983 Boston Marathon. *(Steven E. Sutton/Duomo)*

Early in the 1984 Olympic trials in Olympia, Washington, running with Betty Jo Springs. *(Sailer/McManus)*

Top: My close adviser Bob Sevene at the Olympic trials.

Winning the Olympic trials in 2:31.04. I was crying.
(*Tom Treick*, The Oregonian)

Late in the Olympic Marathon I see on the building ahead a mural of me winning the 1983 Boston Marathon. That's Bill Rodgers with the headphones, doing TV commentary. *(Los Angeles* Times)

Left: The end of the Olympic Marathon. I was really charged up. *(David Madison/ Duomo)*

Right: The victory lap in the Los Angeles Coliseum. *(Los Angeles* Times*)*

On the victory stand with Rosa Mota (third place) and Ingrid Kristiansen
(second).

The start of the 1985 Tufts 10k. (*Jeff Johnson*)

Top: Steve Jones and I won the 1985 America's Marathon in Chicago. *(Sailer/McManus)*

Above: Dinner after the Chicago Marathon, with my husband, Scott Samuelson, and my parents.

Top: Part of my family at our island summer home. First row, my sister-in-law Holly Benoit, my brother John, and my father; second row, my brother Andy, his wife, Stevie, and my husband, Scott; third row, Mom. (My brother Peter didn't make it into this picture.)

Above: Jeff Drenth and I after winning the Trevira Twosome in New York's Central Park, April 1986. Tragically, Jeff died of unknown causes a few weeks later. *(David Getlen)*

Near the cove by our home in Freeport, Maine. *(David Keith)*

and shattered. In 1975 Jacqueline Hansen became the first woman to run the marathon in less than two hours and forty minutes. Five years later, she wrote in an unpublished manuscript: "Five women ran under 2:40 in the Avon Marathon in London this August (1980). . . . In a single weekend (6–7 September) there were five sub-2:35 performances." In fourteen years women had gained not only acceptance, but the admiration and respect of people who'd tried to push them off the roads.

Jacqueline, who is still running, took a substantial role in pressuring the International Olympic Committee to sanction the women's marathon for the 1984 Games. She began her assault in the 1970s but was politely ignored by the officials, who apparently hadn't noticed the changing times. They seemed to be stuck back in the bad old days when women were thought to be too delicate to run more than 1,500 meters. Jacqueline, with help from pioneer runners and current stars, barraged the IOC, the International Amateur Athletic Federation, and the Los Angeles Olympic Organizing Committee with letters and well-reasoned pleas. The result was the first women's Olympic Marathon in 1984. Jacqueline and the others didn't give up there, however: at the 1988 Summer Games in Seoul, South Korea, women will also compete in the 10,000-meter event.

I knew about Jacqueline and Kathy, Bobbi and Nina in 1976, and I admired them. Bobbi is a runner, lawyer, and sculptor (she made the trophy I received for winning the first American Olympic Trials—a work of art I would have been more than proud to buy). Jacqueline is a writer, runner, and mother. Nina is as involved in the sport today as she ever was. And Katherine, now a journalist and TV commentator, went from her Boston debut to other world-class races; from there she joined Avon's promotion department. She convinced the cosmetic company to take a chance on marathons just for women—the Avon International Marathon Series.

These women made it possible for Grete, Ingrid, Mary Slaney, Rosa Mota, and me to compete in the sport we love. Mary herself—the erstwhile "Little Mary Decker," whose phenomenal talent made itself apparent so early in life—was a heroine to me. I clipped articles about her wherever I found them. But even she, who began running as a young teenager, owes something to the tireless women who preceded us. She and I didn't have to sit in or suffer the indignity of being told we couldn't possibly run with men.

Even in 1976 I was grateful for the progress that had been made, though I still didn't consider myself a likely candidate for a long career in running. There was no such thing for women. My generation of runners still had to contend with the fact that we couldn't expect to support ourselves as athletes, but at the same time, we couldn't excel unless we trained full time. So I figured I'd run in college, then keep going as long as I could until I simply had to pursue another career or starve. I've always been grateful for that uncertainty: it was a daily reminder that I must become a well-rounded person in order to survive the loss of running that could occur anytime. I think all of us who came up in the 1970s shared that good fortune. We didn't run ourselves into the ground, as so many talented young runners are doing today in pursuit of the big money, because there wasn't any money. It seemed like ill fortune at the time—and believe me, I'm all for money in running; I couldn't have trained to my peak physical condition while working at another job—but, like most disappointments, it has had its payoff. We've become real people, not just runners.

At the start of my sophomore year at Bowdoin, I could feel myself gathering strength as an athlete. The August win in

Falmouth had given me some pause because of the press attention. I wasn't anxious to risk an invasion of privacy, but running was irresistible. I just kept at it, hoping I'd be able to handle anything that came my way.

Within the year I would meet my future husband, go off to live in a different part of America, make myself too ill to run, and scurry back to Maine to heal. I went with the flow like a starfish that has to ride a thousand waves before finally ending up in the calm shallows.

SIX

Scott Samuelson entered Bowdoin as a freshman when I was a sophomore. We met during fraternity rush week. I was standing in the living room at DKE, talking to someone and forming silent opinions about the people I'd met so far, when Scott came up the stairs from the basement. The staircase was on the other side of the room, but I saw him right away—he is so tall that I can always find him in a crowd. I can't say it was love at first sight because I know how complicated love is; there was something there, though. I thought about lifting my drink to my mouth but my arm stopped in the middle of the journey and I stood there with my mouth hanging open. It was still waiting for the drink. Since I've been known to "space out" at various times—through exhaustion, concentration, or both—my behavior was not especially strange. But I pulled myself together quickly and chatted with him.

Scott decided not to join a fraternity that semester, but we had biology class together and he was on the indoor track team, so I got to see him often. I think we each recognized the attraction and, both being Yankees, didn't want to push it. If it was destined for us to get together, fine. Of course I helped destiny out once in a while—I sat near him in class and went to many of his meets.

Sports are a great outlet for the emotions you don't necessarily want to show undisguised. I went to see Scott compete in a meet at Bates College early in the spring semester. Bowdoin and Bates were evenly matched, and it came down to the pole vault to decide the meet: Scott and his friend Gig Leadbetter against two Bates vaulters. Bowdoin had to take first and second to win. Calm, philosophical Scott was pacing around under the pressure—which is how I know he understands what I'm going through before a race—but he handled things beautifully and took second place. Gig was first. That night there was a big party, and under the guise of raving about his afternoon's performance, I told Scott how wonderful he was. I think he heard what I really meant to say, but he, too, was able to hide behind the track meet. Ours was a gentle relationship from the start; we understood each other.

During this semester, many of my friends were making plans to spend their junior year elsewhere. Some wanted to attend small colleges in New England, others were anxious to go abroad. I wasn't considering a move at the beginning of the semester: Bowdoin was where I wanted to be, and I couldn't see going to Europe and missing the track and cross-country seasons here.

But throughout the winter I ran into Julie Shea at different meets—the Millrose Games, the AAU indoor championships, and other, smaller meets—and she would always ask if I'd consider coming to North Carolina State. The more she talked, the more interested I got.

The previous summer a number of college coaches had written me. Because my race results were posted under the

Liberty A.C. banner, they thought I was a high school senior. There were no outright scholarship offers, but most suggested I might qualify for one if I decided to continue running at the college level.

A running scholarship was tempting. Bowdoin was an expensive school; my parents sacrificed to send me there. The idea of not costing them anything for a year was attractive. I was never sure that they approved of all my running, and I wondered if they'd appreciate it more if I made it work for me. Leaving my parents' feelings aside, I thought about my goals as an athlete. The new Bowdoin running club was okay, but it wasn't a sanctioned team within the Association of Intercollegiate Athletics for Women (AIAW). And I had lingering doubts about my chances of making it into world-class running without more coaching. I didn't know what I needed, but I wanted to look at all the possible options.

At Julie's behest Russ Combs, the N.C. State women's coach, called; we talked, and later I was offered a scholarship for the following academic year.

I like to claim that I went from a school with thirteen hundred students to one with thirteen thousand, but I don't know how accurate that is. The difference was enormous, at any rate: there might have been thirteen million students, the school seemed so huge. It was like going from Portland to New York—immediately overwhelming.

Mike Brust, a fellow runner from Bowdoin, picked me up at the 1977 Falmouth Road Race (which I lost to Kim Merritt) and drove me to Raleigh. We crawled along the eastern seaboard, stopping at friends' houses in New Jersey and Washington, but my arrival couldn't be put off forever. Mike helped me carry my things into the dorm and left quickly; never have I felt so alone. I missed Maine and the ocean instantly and never stopped missing them all the time I spent away.

For once I really regretted being late. My roommate had taken the place over. Her posters were on the walls, her books were on the shelves, her clothes were in the top drawers, and her sheets were on the best bed. I was so intimidated and unhappy that I didn't dream of objecting. She was a southerner, this was her turf, and I felt I shouldn't raise any objections.

She was the first person in her family to go to college; she wanted to be an engineer. I respected the commitment made by her whole family, but there were times when I felt crushed under it. When I wanted a window cracked at night and she didn't, or when I had to sleep and she had to have the lights on to study, I lost. She didn't understand my needs as an athlete and I didn't stick up for myself.

I survived at N.C. State because I was an athlete. We alone were eligible for school dining; everyone else had either to cook in toaster ovens and hot plates in their rooms or go out three times a day for fast food. We ate at the Case Athletic Center and were pampered, by general university standards. Beyond that bit of good luck, I also had an identity as a runner. As always, belonging to a team made me feel more comfortable. Once my race results began to be published locally, the students in my classes recognized me and some of my professors took an interest in me. I was lucky—most of the kids in my dorm had no real identity in the larger university setting aside from their social security numbers. Our grades were posted next to those numbers; I must have been the only student from Maine, because my number stood out and everybody knew which grades were mine. It gave me an incentive to do well in class.

At Bowdoin my professors knew my name. In classes at State I was one of forty, fifty, a hundred students or more; my teachers there didn't stop me on the quad to reprimand me for a bad test score or compliment me on a good one. The

Bowdoin faculty didn't allow anonymity among students; for every professor who was formal and distant, there were two who invited you to have coffee, wine, and cheese with some well-chosen friends. But State was too big to work that way.

I lost a big chunk of naiveté there. I had a reputation as a scholar-athlete, and while taking tests I would be surrounded by students who hoped to get a look at my paper. I really believe in academic honor codes and thought everyone else did too. There were people on the faculty, assigned to proctor exams, who would sit at a desk in the front of the room holding up newspapers so they couldn't see the cheating. I took tests hunched over my blue books like Croesus over his gold.

One thing I loved doing at State was selling programs at football and basketball games. To go from little Bowdoin, where football games were mostly an excuse to socialize, to a big school in the Atlantic Coast Conference was eye-opening. The Wolfpack played in a big stadium, but the stands were filled for every home game. On one side of the arena almost every spectator would be dressed in N.C. State red; on the other side there'd be a powder-blue sea for Carolina, a navy one for Duke, or whatever. I couldn't believe how loyal and enthusiastic ACC students and alumni were. At State they thought nothing of camping out all night to get tickets to an important game—and in basketball season, that could mean surviving horrible weather. But the ACC was especially competitive that year—Duke went to the NCAA basketball finals—so students risked colds and flu to see the conference games. As a program seller, I never had to wait in long lines. That, and the good money I earned, made the games highlights of my routine.

The classwork wasn't as strenuous as at Bowdoin, though I tried to take advantage of the school's specialties in the sciences, particularly botany. Even adding an extra course each semester was manageable. That was a good thing, because I was working my tail off on the track.

I missed New England so much that I asked Russ Combs for permission to run in extra road races if they didn't conflict with college cross-country meets—soon I was taking any opportunity to leave the campus. Most students packed off for somewhere else on Saturday and Sunday, so I wasn't missing much social life. It was always a relief to escape from the smell of greasy food in the dorms, and though the travel wore me down, I slept better on the road than I did on campus. There were no drunk, lonely boys howling on the quad just to hear themselves howl.

Luckily, I was getting good enough for race sponsors to pick up some of my expenses. I met Pam Magee, who worked with women athletes for Nike, in the fall semester of 1977. In the months to come I eased into a relationship with Nike that continues to this writing. Pam made sure that decision makers at Nike were aware of my progress, for which I was grateful. I needed frequent reassurance that there would be life after N.C. State.

My days were monotonous. I ran, went to class, and studied. Running in practice every day with Julie Shea and her younger sister Mary was difficult because Julie liked to turn every practice into a race. She hated to lose. If I beat her— in practice or in a meet—she would turn subsequent workouts into gritty duels. I had never trained with so much intensity. I think it is necessary to test yourself against other runners as part of training, but my method has been to worry about my times and try to beat myself before I become concerned about the competition. Julie's need for racelike conditions first dumbfounded, then annoyed me. I didn't back away from her challenges, so maybe I was as guilty as she.

But I dreaded our daily competition, even though we were great pals off the track. I've lost touch with Julie in the ensuing years as she has apparently slipped away from competitive running. She pushed herself awfully hard when she was young; she deserves to do something else for a while— no doubt she was tired of being a runner to the exclusion of all else. I miss seeing her, though I don't miss her on the track. She exhausted me.

The worst thing about my first semester at State was that I got into a rut: nine out of ten of the people I associated with were runners. I finally noticed the problem when I went home for Christmas and caught up with my nonrunning friends. I'd forgotten there was a whole world that didn't care about pulled muscles and split times.

I returned to Raleigh with a new attitude, but I had to take a few steps back before I could move forward. I was determined to make some friends away from track. I decided not to eat with my teammates at the Case Center; I took the money allotted for meals and tried to feed myself. That turned out to be a disaster: I couldn't cook balanced meals in my room and there wasn't enough money to eat out all the time. I gained a lot of weight, because I would take in the All-You-Can-Eat specials at local restaurants. Every night on my way home from the library I would stop for two or three scoops of the inexpensive, delicious ice cream made by the agricultural students.

Finally, feeling fat and isolated, I found Barb Walker, who was from New Jersey. When I heard her speak I thought, "At last, somebody who'll understand why I feel like a foreigner here." She took me in hand and introduced me to her friends. Some were tennis players, like Barb, but not all. I admit I was surprised at the number of artistic, entertaining people Barb knew. Where had they been all this time? The better question, of course, was where had I been?

Barb was a big help in the coming months. I got very sick shortly after I met her, and her apartment became my refuge. Even though my new roommate was a freshman who never said boo, I still didn't feel at home in the mammoth dorm. Barb always had a free bed for me to use if I wasn't feeling well or if I just had to get away overnight. It was great to have a friend so far away from home.

My illness came on slowly. I'd been feeling sluggish since returning from vacation, but I put that down to my diet, which was high in fat from all the ice cream. I first realized that somehing else was wrong at the AAU indoor championships in February. I ran the 3,000 and my time was terrible. The year before I had been blown away in the same race, not even placing in the top ten, but I expected to do much better after a year of hard training. Back in my New York hotel I discovered I had a fever. That meant I could put the race behind me and get some sleep—it wasn't my fault. My times in both practice and competition were off for a month: I thought it was because I had run with the fever.

I was sure I was back to normal at a meet at the University of Virginia in April. We'd run outside in that sweet, crisp spring air and I was happy with my performances, winning one event and placing high with a personal record in another. On the bus to Raleigh, however, fatigue struck again. I'm not talking about the pleasant weariness that comes from using a conditioned body to its best ends, but about the kind of exhaustion that makes it difficult to move your eyes. I was so tired I couldn't lift my head off the seat; a teammate had to help me stand.

The next day I skipped practice and slept all day, thinking I could kick the exhaustion. Monday I felt well enough to go to class, but I had a persistent sore throat all week. I ignored it.

The Big Three meet was held the following Friday, with

State, Duke, and North Carolina participating. The local press gave it a big buildup; supposedly, Julie and I and Ellison Goodall of Duke would be trying to break ten minutes for two miles. I slept at Barb's apartment the night before the meet so no one could find me and ask how I thought I'd do. If I know I'm going to do well I don't want to jinx it by talking about it, and if I have no idea, saying so sounds like a cop-out. I always try to disappear before a big race.

When I awoke Friday, the bedsheets were literally soaked in sweat. I knew I was running a high fever but didn't dare take my temperature. If I was sick it was my fault—I shouldn't have traveled so much and shouldn't have tried to save money cooking for myself. I couldn't let my team down by not running. I literally pulled myself out of bed, and with Barb's help (though she objected all the way) I got to the track.

I heard the starter's gun go off in one distorted sound wave, like a whale song heard underwater from a half mile away. I ran on instinct, I suppose, but I remember wanting to drop out at once. The scholarship loomed over my head as the State athletic director yelled, "Come on, Benoit, move!" What was he thinking? I didn't know, but I tried to move. I owed them something.

I guess there wouldn't have been any shame in dropping out. But I knew leaving one race would make it easier to leave another and still another. To this day I have finished every race I started, no matter how badly I've been running. You could call it pride, but it's really fear—I'm afraid to relax my standards. So I kept running that day and even managed to stay on my feet until Barb deposited me back in my dorm bed. Then I collapsed for two days with a 104-degree fever.

I went to my Monday morning class feeling dizzy and sick. There is nothing like being sick away from home to make you feel as if you've hit bottom. Nobody cares the way someone in your family would care. And if you become ill in an uncomfortable environment, it's like being given up for dead. I was afraid I'd faint if I tried to make it through the day, so I went from my class to the infirmary. A doctor bawled me out for being a stoic and told me I had mononucleosis. He wanted to put me in bed then and there, but he let me leave when I begged for the chance to clear up some commitments. I went to each of my professors and made arrangements to get assignments: I called a few friends to let them know where I'd be, then slept for a week in the infirmary.

I missed the remainder of the outdoor track season and had to postpone my final exams. It was the logical ending to a difficult year. What made it worse was that I knew I'd brought it on myself by not eating well and by overdoing. I've never been a fanatic on the subject of training diets; I just try to be sensible. I eat plenty of fruits and vegetables, whole grains, fish, chicken, cheese, and sweets in moderation. I try not to consume anything unusual in the week before a race. Even though I run my best training loops after Mexican food I can't bring myself to eat it the night before a marathon. Otherwise, I eat what I crave because my body knows itself best. My mother served balanced meals at home, and when I lost sight of those guidelines I got into trouble. This was the first time I abused myself that way, but unfortunately it wasn't the last. I've suffered from anemia a couple of times because I haven't found the time to eat properly. I always feel like an idiot when I realize that, once again, I've let myself get into a funk for the lack of some basic good food.

At least I recovered from the mono quickly: I had caught the variety that didn't linger. I took my exams and couldn't wait to get out of Raleigh. Before I left, Russ Combs asked if I would think about coming back for another semester. I should have said no outright, but I hung my head and mumbled something negative. I wanted to get back to Maine; I didn't want to hurt anyone's feelings.

That summer I worked in a greenhouse in Cape Elizabeth. I had a mo-ped to get back and forth from work; it took almost as much courage to ride that machine on the narrow roads as it did to run on them. I ran six miles or so every morning, then stood on my feet all day: I might not have been able to face an evening run if it hadn't been for the companionship of Bruce Bickford. He is one of Maine's finest runners—in 1985 he was ranked number one in the world in the 10,000. That summer he came up from Northeastern University to paint houses and train with another outstanding Maine runner, Kenny Flanders. Every afternoon when I got home from work Bruce and I went out running. I think I owe my fast recovery to him. Because he was so good at pacing me, because he helped me find new depths of strength in myself, I was physically back to normal by July, and I won the Falmouth race in August.

Two other people actively supported my comeback that summer: Mom and Scott. As I built up my strength Bruce and I ran farther and farther together—by the end of July it was impossible to predict when I would feel like coming home. Mom held dinner for me so I could get that second run in. It was a family custom that we all ate dinner together no matter what: it was up to the kids to be home on time. Mom bent the rules for me, obviously knowing how important the evening run was to my confidence level. That she would make any sort of concession to my running meant a great deal to me.

Scott had decided to join DKE at the beginning of the school year. I got an invitation to the initiation while I was at

N.C. State, the perfect excuse to write to him. We were still tiptoeing around the idea that we really liked each other. I told him I thought he'd made a great choice, and that DKE was lucky to get him. He answered my letter. I watched the calendar before I wrote again, ticking off a couple of weeks so I wouldn't look too anxious—and on it went throughout the year in much the same way.

Scott had a job with a construction crew in Hanover, New Hampshire, that summer, and he came over to Cape Elizabeth a few times. Though I always had hope that the relationship might take off, it didn't. We spent most of our time with groups of vacationing Bowdoin students. I couldn't tell whether Scott really liked me or not—he likes everybody. Now that we're married and I've had a chance to observe him closely for a couple of years, I know that if we are in a group and one person seems to be removed from the conversation, Scott will eventually pull that person in. I can almost time him. Scott is sincere: he isn't one of those people who take your hand, ask you an earnest question, and gaze impatiently over your head while you answer. He's like a human can opener—he has to know what's going on inside your head. His personal generosity made me wonder, sometimes, just how special I was to him. I knew he respected me, and that was enough to give me a boost in my training. He participated in my comeback without even knowing it. We almost never talked about running, but when we did it was because Scott sensed I was frustrated about something and needed to get it out.

Not knowing how things stood between Scott and me made me more vulnerable to the weekly calls I was getting from N.C. State. Russ Combs would phone and say, "You know, we really have a shot at the championship if you'll come back this fall." Then I heard from Jim Wescott, the men's coach, a New Hampshire native to whom I had run in many fits of homesickness during the past year. They got to me after a while. I agreed to return under two conditions: that I would still be free to compete outside of North Carolina as long as my schedule didn't conflict with the team's; and that they wouldn't try to persuade me to return for yet another semester. Russ honored both conditions.

I didn't want to leave Maine again, I didn't want to leave Bowdoin and Scott. Bowdoin was home, and my friends there would be returning from their junior years abroad ready to have a terrific final year together. But of course I felt guilty. I had taken State's scholarship and then let them down by getting ill. When I cut through all of the pressure and my apprehension about returning—realizing that Scott didn't figure in it because neither of us had declared anything to the other—one fact remained: if I didn't go back and give them my best, I would feel as if I had left a job undone. So I was satisfied with my decision, however unwelcome it was.

I returned to Raleigh in September and was far happier. My living arrangements were better—I shared a house with some athletes off campus—and I stuck to the university training table. I didn't have to worry about nutrition or illness on a limited budget. The summer had made me fit to do the team some good, so everyone was pleased with me. We finished second at the AIAW National championships in Colorado and I made All-America. We weren't number one, but Russ Combs was right—we did indeed have a shot.

My own running career took off once and for all that autumn. I set a world best at the Bonne Bell 10k on October 9. People in New England and in running circles were familiar with my name prior to the Bonne Bell, but that race gave me more exposure in the national press than I'd had before. I have a wonderful mental picture of Pam Magee standing in the Nike corporate offices saying "See? I told you," and convincing them to sign me up. I have no idea if it actually went that way, but I think she took almost as much pleasure as I did when I began receiving equipment from Nike.

What does my N.C. State experience say about coaching? I didn't improve as a runner until I came home, got well, and trained with Bruce Bickford. He knew how to slow me down: every few minutes I would get ahead of him and he'd yell at me to come back right now, which is what I needed. The workouts with Julie Shea hurt more than they helped, because I wasn't able to pace myself. But at least I had daily updates on the state of my competition, depressing though that could be. And Russ was a good coach. He knew I needed to get away from State frequently for my peace of mind, and he did not insist that I run for him alone. He taught me more about track racing than I could have learned on my own. He gave me the chance to be around people who took running as seriously as I did, and he was enthusiastic about my future.

But N.C. State only strengthened my feeling that I didn't need constant coaching. There were people like Bruce and John Babington who could give me advice about running and count on my attention, but their willingness to let me go my own way without resentment was the priceless part of our relationships. I'm probably a terrible role model for runners coming up in the sport: I don't recommend that they drop their coaches and hit the roads alone. What works for me may not work for others. Most top runners have coaches who've either stayed with them or continued to give them advice from their college offices. I am helped by Bob Sevene of the Athletics West running club: he shows up to run with me in Freeport once in a while and we talk on the phone a few times a week. Sev doesn't tell me how to run; he's more likely to report what Ingrid Kristiansen or Lynn Jennings is up to. That, for me, is excellent coaching, the kind of stuff that makes me force myself to train in a cold drizzle. If N.C. State did nothing else for me, it taught me I could rely on myself and a few well-chosen motivators.

An AIAW-approved team was organized at Bowdoin while I was in North Carolina (wouldn't you know), so now I could run for Bowdoin in intercollegiate competition. Right away there was a conflict. I wanted to participate in the Bermuda 10k in January, but Bowdoin had a meet with Bates two days later. I convinced Frank Sabasteanski to let me go by promising to be back for the Bates meet without fail.

By now I was accustomed to missing weekends at school, but I felt funny about leaving Bowdoin almost before I had unpacked. Still, it was an exciting weekend on the island—there were two races held in two days, the 10k on Saturday followed by a marathon on Sunday. In those days I loved running in Bermuda; now there are too many cars. In 1979 I could find places where cars wouldn't run me off the road. I was in a great mood going into the race.

Ten kilometers is a good distance for me. I've never really had the ability to sprint at the end of a race, but I do have stamina. As long as I'm feeling well I should be able to stay in a race with anybody. The 10k is made for someone with strength. I knew I had plenty of that after running with Bruce Bickford all summer and gradually lengthening my workouts through the fall. I was running eighty to ninety miles per week at that time. I left the starting line with a confidence that is hard to describe. It isn't euphoria, exactly, and it isn't overconfidence. It's as if I'm an inventor; I created this body and now I'm watching it work. Any glitches in the moving parts? (No.) Are the pumps and valves leaking? (No.) Is there too much stress anywhere? (Not yet.) The invention can be monitored for just so long before the creator either begins to trust it or watches it break down. There's a point in every race, and it's different in each, where I realize that my body is either going to make it to the end in fine style or be in trouble. Once that point is passed I start making decisions to account for the condition of the machine. That day in Bermuda, despite a slightly sore heel, I knew things were right from the beginning. I won the race and beat Julie Shea for the first time at that distance.

I wasn't gunning for Julie—I aim for times, not people—but I knew it was an important win. I had passed another psychological milestone, like running the sub–five-minute mile or setting the state record in high school. If I could run with Julie Shea at this distance, that was one thing. If I could run faster, I would keep it up and get better. Given proof that I can do something once, I'm always tempted to stick to it until I've done as well as I can. Thus, the goals I set sometimes seem impossible to obtain—I try to leave myself with something to shoot for. It is important that I not compromise the big goals that I set for myself. Intermediate goals keep me honest and on track in accomplishing bigger goals.

Most of the people in the race, including Bruce, were staying to watch the marathon. My flight to Maine wasn't until late Monday morning; the meet at Bates was Monday evening. On Sunday I got out of bed early and went for a run with Ellison Goodall. "Hey," she said as we rounded a dark bay, "why don't we enter the marathon?"

At first I thought she was crazy. The wind had died down overnight but picked up again in the morning, bringing rain clouds in with it. But weather or no weather, heel or no heel,

I was pumped up. I thought it might be fun to tear along with the pack for a while and drop out when I got tired. We ran to the registration booth and were just in time to pin on our numbers before the race started.

Adrenaline took over from reason. I never got tired. There was one moment when the inventor checked all systems and asked "Do we know what we're doing?" and I almost stopped; but then my body calmly explained that I might as well finish, since I wouldn't be able to get a ride back to the hotel until the "meat wagon," the van that was following the last runner, picked us up and brought us to the finish line. From then on I slogged through the light rain, my shirt soaking in the moisture and making me feel as if I were covered in a layer of cold slime. When I didn't want to think about my foolishness I concentrated on the runners ahead of me. I passed the time watching their feet rise and fall, trying to keep the time within catching range. Before I knew it I had overtaken all but one of the women: I ran my first marathon in 2:50.54, fast enough to qualify for the Boston Marathon in April.

At dinner that evening I arranged to meet Bruce and some others for a jog the next morning. There was no sense in trying to run, but jogging might help take the kinks out of our legs. We met as planned, though I was limping because my heel had become stiff overnight. As we shuffled along, I knew something was very wrong. My calves and thighs loosened up relatively well, but the heel was killing me. It didn't take Bruce long to notice my limp. He told me to call it a day. I went back to the hotel and packed my bags for the return home. I got on my plane, hoping the stiffness and soreness in the heel would go away when I had time to nurse it.

I arrived in Portland late that afternoon and was met by

some guys from the track team. We went straight to Bates: I barely had time to warm up. Bates is another small New England college that at the time had an old track featuring tight turns—I knew my left heel wouldn't be able to handle the small track wearing spikes, so I put on my training shoes.

Why didn't I go to Coach Sabasteanski and say, "Look, Sabe, I hurt myself in Bermuda and you'll have to get along without me"? After all, I wasn't on scholarship anymore; I didn't have to earn my keep. But he had let me go to Bermuda on the strength of my promise to run this meet, so I had to run. I honestly thought I could take care of my heel by resting it in the coming week. And I didn't want to admit that I couldn't handle running both for Bowdoin and on my own.

But the Bates meet was a mistake. To add insult to injury, I didn't place as expected and Bowdoin lost. I should have given the team more points. The heel didn't improve after that. I tried to train with it, but the pain was too insistent.

After a few days of frustration I went to Boston and John Babington took me to see Dr. Robert Leach, an orthopedic surgeon and sports medicine specialist at University Hospital who has since become my link to health. After examining me in his hospital office he led me upstairs, saying "I want to show you what will happen to you if you don't watch it."

We went into a room where Jos Hermans, the Dutch runner who still holds the world record for the hour track run, was recuperating from surgery on both his heels. Jos allowed himself to be exhibited, lying there with two casts on his feet. Seeing him scared me into doing what I was told: Dr. Leach said I had to take time off if I wanted my heel to mend properly. It was frustrating advice after winning the 10k and running my first marathon—I was champing for more, but I stopped for a few weeks. I remember going to Bowdoin's indoor track and watching the athletes work out like a prisoner from behind tall bars; I desperately wanted to run. I wasn't used to doing the prudent thing where injuries were concerned, but Leach's reputation for knowing his business kept me from being stupid.

That was the first of the many problems I've had with my Achilles tendons. I couldn't know that I would later be haunted by chronic heel injuries; I hoped this episode was isolated. When I was rested I started running harder than ever and the tendon seemed to be healed. I tested myself at some AAU indoor meets that winter and performed to my satisfaction.

In March I went before a Bowdoin faculty committee to ask for permission to graduate with my class that spring. Every student was supposed to spend the last two semesters in residence to be eligible for graduation. I had only spent one of these two required semesters in residence, as I had felt compelled to return to N.C. State for an extra semester senior year. I hoped they would make an exception for me, but the committee stood by the rule, and I was told that the soonest I could graduate would be January 1980.

I thought about taking a leave of absence and coming back to graduate when I had the time. Competition over the summer would lose some of its zest if I had an extra semester of school hanging over my head. I wanted to graduate with my friends. Sitting in the Union, listening to my classmates talk about graduate schools and jobs, I felt left out. Next fall I'd be marking time. My friends were getting on with their lives, while I was . . . running. I passed a large chunk of each day running in circles. My training was done in loops: out to the ocean and back, in circles around Brunswick, and over to Freeport. No matter where I went I always ended up back where I started; there was no indisputably forward motion in my life.

I didn't pay as much attention as I should have to people like Sam Butcher, who taught chemistry and environmental studies. He and I used to run together and talk about the environment. It was obvious that he respected my athletic pursuits. "But," I thought, "he's a runner himself. People who don't run can't think much of me. Why should a future doctor, somebody who's going to do something really worthwhile, have any respect for me?"

I suppose I was angry with Bowdoin for refusing to let me graduate because the reasoning hit close to home. Deep down I thought they were right: my running wasn't important enough to bend a rule. I wasn't accomplishing anything an academic institution regarded as special.

Looking back on it now, I can see how this setback helped me. When you have an occupation like mine—self-contained, lonely work that allows you to call yourself boss—you have to make a solid commitment to it. No one in this world would be adversely affected if I stopped running tomorrow; I might get a few calls from people wondering what happened, but I'm not part of a giant corporate machine. I do have corporate sponsors who'd like to see me run for many years to come, but if I didn't they'd get over it. Nobody relies on me to do my job except me: I had to learn to rely on myself. Bowdoin's attitude toward my running made me ponder the possibility of giving it up. I couldn't see where it was taking me anyway, since the sport wasn't overloaded with money in those days. But when the question reached my heart, when I stepped back and said "So what?" the answer was clear. All I could do was tell myself to keep going. If my running was of little consequence to others, it would always be important to me. I had my goals. If I didn't try to reach them I'd be—that dreaded word again—a quitter. I swallowed the news from the faculty committee, learned to be happy for my graduating friends, and tried to look ahead.

And there was consolation in staying at school. I'd come back from State, taken one look at Scott, and known it was time for us to get serious. We were living in the same apartment complex that semester and met frequently for lunch. Scott was on a sugared-cereal kick for a while and I gave him a hard time about that until he caught me wolfing some Boo-Berry I'd left at his place as a present. I still didn't have money for lavish gifts, but once in a while I'd surprise Scott with a box of Sugar Smacks and he would leave me a thank-you note in Alpha-Bit letters.

We started to call each other M.D., for Major Distraction. We both had tons of schoolwork and found it hard to concentrate even when separated. But we managed, mostly by making our time together count. I wasn't shy about letting him know how I felt anymore. Right after the Bermuda races we went together to a semiformal dance. When I went to his apartment to pick him up he was in the last stages of dressing but was still undecided about his tie. He owned the loudest, worst ties I've ever seen. I went right to the closet and picked out the wildest one of the bunch. I think we knew then that we were destined to be soulmates forever.

One thing we didn't do together often—and still don't, when I can help it—was run. I remember going out for a easy nine-mile run with him one day. For the first few miles he was totally bored. He kicked a stone along in front of him; he got hot and took off his shirt, then balled it up and began throwing it in the air and catching it. I tried to get mad at him for being such a geek while I was working, but I was laughing too hard. At six miles he dropped behind me and I heard an awful moan. "Ooooo," he said, "oooo, Joan, I've got cramps." I turned around and he was running along with his arms straight up in the air, fighting a side stitch. It served him right for fooling around. I kept going and he walked back to campus.

Now he does the same thing when we swim together. He won't do the crawl because he can't see where he's going, so he swims breaststroke, which is boring for him. About halfway through my mile workout I'll look up and Scott will be fooling around with some cannonballs. It makes me laugh and I could rap him sometimes.

Given our troubles in exercising together, Scott pretty much went his own way. He always had a million and one things on his mind anyway. If I asked him what he'd be doing while I was out on my afternoon run he'd reel off a list of goals that couldn't have been met by twenty people. I usually left him experimenting with ferrets, which was required for his psychobiology degree. We were an unusual couple: I ran, he watched ferrets and practiced the pole vault.

It took me a month or so to settle down after being told I wouldn't graduate, but my commitment to running was stronger than ever. I began to train for the Boston Marathon. Since that was the most prestigious marathon in America, I very much wanted to run there. Andrea Cayer would have said it was a glory event; but I wasn't in it for the glory. I just wanted to see how well I could do when I seriously prepared for a marathon. I'd had so many good experiences in races in and around Boston that it seemed like a good place to do some experimenting.

Bill Rodgers and Patti Lyons were the favorites in 1979. Bill was at the apex of his brilliant career. Patti had good days and bad days; it was difficult to predict how she'd finish, but she'd been enjoying a successful year so far.

Once I snapped out of my gloom I realized I was in a position to run well. My training loops went faster and faster, even though I was increasing my mileage. I ran about a hundred miles the week before the Boston race and knew I was in great shape.

April 16 was cold and drizzly. I hate running in rain, wind, and humidity now, but then I was too inexperienced to know the difference. The runners gathered in Hopkinton, west of Boston, and went through their pre-race routines in the rain—I watched the top runners bounce and shiver with nerves. But it was all a lark for me. Now I can't imagine being so calm before a marathon: the pressure to win is crushing. But I was out for a good time that year. It was a private test, Joan running for Joan's sake. I could afford to be peaceful. I was about six rows deep when the gun went off, but I got my legs moving and dug in to concentrate despite all the commotion (helicopters overhead, photographers on utility trucks, fans, etc.). All I promised myself was that I'd run as far as I could.

I had my choice of wardrobe for the marathon. Since high school I'd worn the Liberty, N.C. State, or Bowdoin uniform, depending upon which team I was representing; at Boston I could wear Liberty's or Bowdoin's colors. I was still ticked off at the faculty committee, but I remembered a classic Bowdoin story. Dick Henderson, a cross-country captain, had run Boston one year wearing a Bowdoin singlet. Out on the course somebody yelled, "Hey, Bowdoin, you're a long way from Waterville!"—the home of archrival Colby College. I decided to put Bowdoin on the map if I could. I'd tell them where Bowdoin was. And in that moment of loyalty, I realized I loved the college in spite of the committee.

In his novel *The Sportswriter*, Richard Ford writes: "Athletes probably think and feel the fewest things of anyone at important times—their training sees to that—though even they can be counted on to have more than one thing in their mind at a time."

This may account for the random memories I have of this race. I was thinking about what I might have for dinner while also worrying about how many classes I was missing at Bowdoin. I took the lead about two-thirds of the way through the race on the infamous Heartbreak Hill and held it the rest of way. There was a part of me that wanted to believe that I'd been seeing things when I passed Patti Lyons: the lead is a huge responsibility. But I knew the TV cameras were trained on me from about mile eighteen on and I realized something special was happening. I was afraid of blowing up, I guess, but I hardly acknowledged the fear. As we were passing Heartbreak Hill, I barely noticed the incline. At this point I was sure I'd be fine to the end. I was running in a pack of men and I was completely comfortable.

At mile twenty-three or so somebody came out of the crowd and ran along with me for a few seconds. He said he was a Bowdoin DKE; I didn't catch the name or the class. In one hand he held a beer, in the other, a Red Sox cap. He said, "Either wear the cap or chug the beer," so I grabbed the cap and put it on backward. From then on the Boston people were with me. Patti was a local and I'm sure most of the spectators wanted her to win, but I had a long lead by then. Seeing Bowdoin written across my chest and the Red Sox cap on my head, the spectators took my victory with grace, even enthusiasm. They've since made Boston feel like a second home.

My time was 2:35:15, which looks slow these days. As Bill Rodgers said in his post-race interview, that time would have won the 1938 men's marathon. It was a new American and course record for women.

After I crossed the line I entered a whirlwind. I guess no one expected me to win the race, because even the veteran reporters seemed excited. The press ringed me as I tried to make my way to the dressing rooms and fired question after question. I don't remember saying anything intelligible; I was glad to be in the arms of two burly Boston policemen, who looked as if they'd be willing to carry me up over their heads if necessary to break the media blockade. Their mission was to get me atop the victory stand to accept the laurel wreath from the mayor's wife.

Before facing the press formally I had a few minutes to towel down and dress in borrowed clothes in a makeshift room in the Prudential Center parking lot, while a doctor followed me around to see if I was going to collapse. There were no shower facilities so I became chilled and began to shiver. The bottoms of my feet were sore, as if I'd been walking on blazing-hot tar.

After the press conference and a hot shower I went to *the* runners' mecca—the nearby Eliot Lounge—to celebrate with countless other runners. Tommy Leonard, the bartender at the Eliot Lounge, has long been a friend of running and runners. The walls of the lounge are covered with pictures of past runners of the Boston Marathon as well as most of New England's greatest runners. Needless to say, I didn't buy anything that night. I relaxed in the gigantic, friendly crowd, even though the noise level rose until I was sure we could be heard back in Maine. I wish I had a dollar bill for every slightly drunken person who stuck his face in mine and yelled, "You did great!" I'd scream "Thank you!" and add to the uproar.

The next morning I flew to Portland. I had to meet my ride on the lower level of the airport, and as I went down the stairs a man stopped me and asked if I needed a wheelchair.

I did hurt. In Cape Elizabeth that afternoon I decided to do some washing before heading back to school. My parents' laundry room was in the basement, so I tried to avoid the tender spots on my feet while hobbling up and down the stairs. I was grateful for the chance to walk the stiffness out of my legs: massage was not an option for me at that point.

My clean clothes and I were back at Bowdoin by dinnertime. As I walked into the dining room everyone stood and clapped. This was a great moment in my life; not because I enjoy being celebrated, but because it showed me that my Bowdoin friends respected my running. In my anger at the faculty committee I had become just insecure enough to forget that Bowdoin's mission was to turn out individuals. The college no more expected us to march lockstep in academic ranks than it expected us all to run the Boston Marathon. The ovation brought my sense of purpose back. The college community would always support me if I pursued my running with devotion and sincerity.

Bowdoin President Willard Enteman gave a reception for me at the college four days after the race. The night before, my friend Cathy Fogler took me out to celebrate and we ended up at Howard Johnson's eating fish and chips at three in the morning. By the time the reception began, the guest of honor was tired and emotionally wrung out. It was all too much for me. My mailbox was stuffed with what I thought was my boxmate's graduate school correspondence, but I soon found out it was all for me, mostly from strangers.

Everyone on campus smiled at me. At the reception, when President Enteman gave me a pewter plate and a telegram from President Jimmy Carter, it was all I could do not to break down.

I was saved from tears by a student who ran in from the hall and said, "The President is on the phone."

I pointed to President Enteman. "He's right there," I said. "No, I mean the President of the United States."

I did what people usually do in those circumstances; I said, "Oh sure." But he insisted, so I followed him to the phone and took the call. I kept wondering which of my friends would pull such a trick. After going through several brief conversations with White House officials, however, I realized that the next voice I heard really would be the President's. When he came on, the tone of voice and accent were unmistakable. I don't remember what he said. I could hardly hear him, for one thing, and my brain was overloaded. I couldn't process a conversation with the President of the United States just then. Mrs. Carter spoke to me after her husband, but I don't recall what she talked about, either.

Later there was some controversy when Bill Rodgers was invited to dinner at the White House and I wasn't. Carter told reporters he thought he'd invited me over the telephone. An editorial appeared in a prominent newspaper saying that the President had insulted women everywhere, and I received a formal invitation a few days later. I was very unhappy about the flap. Bill didn't deserve to have his big moment spoiled, and I wasn't crazy about the idea of being an afterthought. But I decided to find a date and go.

Scott firmly declined. Maybe he thought I was kidding, maybe he was uncomfortable being the escort of a so-called celebrity. He respected me as an athlete but didn't make much comment about it. We had dozens of topics to discuss that were more relevant to us. So when he decided he didn't want to go to Washington, I didn't push for an explanation. He honored my need for privacy, so I would honor his feelings. I asked a classmate, Fred Barnes, to come along. Fred was easygoing and I knew he'd get a kick out of the pomp. He'd worked for Senator Abraham Ribicoff the summer before and loved Washington.

The dinner was in honor of Prime Minister Ohira of Japan. My mother insisted that I buy a new dress for the occasion, something I might have thought of myself if I'd been focusing, but I was still walking on air. I got the dress and arranged to spend two nights in Washington with Joan Walker, a friend from Cape Elizabeth. Fred was staying with a Capitol Hill acquaintance whose car we would be borrowing to get to the White House.

Fred arrived at Joan's place to pick me up in an old, beat-up white Mustang. We collected Bill and Ellen Rodgers at their hotel and set off. At the White House gate the guard took a long look at the car and at our formal evening clothes (the guys were in tuxedos) and must have thought, "If these people think they're going to crash a state dinner, they came to the wrong gate." We handed our invitations through the cracked window and he read them under a light. He came back to the car and peered in suspiciously. But he turned out to be a running buff and recognized Bill. I wish I had a picture of our Mustang parked among the black limousines. I'm sure we were a sight.

In the dining area, which was on the outside terrace, there were a hundred or so people already waiting. We were seated a few chairs down from a Japanese couple, and I noticed two other Japanese sitting slightly removed from the table—they turned out to be the Ohiras' translators. A well-known actor was eating handfuls of peanuts out of a bowl, looking bored, elbows on the table. I wondered how he could eat when the President hadn't arrived yet.

I looked down at my silverware and said a short prayer for my table manners. I was hoping Mom's training would take hold and help me through the rough spots. If I had to think about it I knew I'd pick up the wrong fork or something. By the time the President showed up I was almost too paranoid to eat.

We all stood when the doorman announced the Carters. I twisted around to see where they were, and before I knew it, they were at our table. I was sitting next to Rosalynn Carter, across the table from the President. That was a big surprise: I had hoped to get an occasional glimpse of them from across the room and maybe a handshake at the end of the evening. The Prime Minister and his wife were near us, but they were so absorbed with the actor that I didn't have to summon my international manners.

I was nervous enough about the President—when he began to ask thoughtful, serious questions about running, I could only stare at him for a few moments. Eventually I tried to answer him in something like complete sentences. Like most people from Maine I wasn't used to calling men "sir," so I'd add the word to the end of my thoughts like a kite tail ("Well, I've been running for about six years . . . sir"). I was pretty relieved when Mrs. Carter took over.

She described the painting and refurbishment they were doing on that wing of the house. I listened and nodded. She said they were worried about the anti-nuke demonstration scheduled for that weekend. She wondered how I felt about nuclear power.

I'd come prepared to discuss the subject, knowing about the demonstration. I told Mrs. Carter that what worried me was the storage problem. I was conerned that the materials used to make the nuclear-waste containers would not outlast the half-life of the radioactive waste. There was a pause, and the First Lady eased away from the topic by raising the idea of alternative energy sources. She had friends in Georgia who'd just built an entirely solar-dependent home. I was delighted to discuss that; I've since put a couple of the design features she mentioned into our house in Freeport.

The Carters left early, but the rest of us were treated to a concert by Bobby Short. I kept hoping Amy Carter would come downstairs and offer to let me see her dollhouses. But when the evening was over the Rodgerses and Fred and I got a wonderful tour of the White House—everything but the Carters' private quarters—from a Secret Service agent.

The next day we flew to Maine—both Fred and I had final exams to take. I was lucky I passed my courses that semester, with all the distractions after Boston. Once finals were out of the way I went on to the AIAW Nationals at Michigan State, where I won the 10,000m in 33:40.7 and finished third in the 3,000m the following day, in 9:20.4.

The attention that came my way after Boston was both flattering and frightening. I worried that I somehow belonged to everybody, that strangers were deciding the course my life would take. I had an awful time saying no to anyone, so my schedule was jammed all the time. The requests for personal appearances came from everywhere. Most of the causes were worthy, but there wasn't enough of me to go around. I felt guilty when I had to say no, but I couldn't do it all.

The week after the marathon I'd gotten a call from a talent agent who said there was a movie role available for an athlete and he was pushing the people in Hollywood to cast me. He asked for a portfolio with photographs of me in a leotard, a tennis outfit, and a cheerleader's uniform. I said I'd try to get around to it soon. Other things were pouring in at that point, so I put the agent's request in the back of my mind.

In early summer he called. "Where are the pictures?" he screamed. "Don't you realize there are a million people out there who want this part and we're practically handing it to you?" I apologized for letting him down and he told me I could take a flying leap (or words to that effect).

I hung up the phone, sat on the floor, and cried. I vowed I would never run another marathon; it just wasn't worth it if I had to deal with such people. The man made me feel that I'd done something horribly wrong—in one swoop I'd ruined my whole life.

In the end the catharsis was good for me. I had to cope with notoriety the same way I'd dealt with doubts about a running career. I weighed the pros and cons and, as usual, found that my desire to run outweighed the problems. It was easier to go back to college for the last semester. Bowdoin was a wall I could hide behind if I needed to.

Though I rested in September, I was still tired when I ran the Bonne Bell in October. I came in third behind Lynn Jennings and Margaret Groos. It wasn't fatigue that beat me, though. I was outclassed, for one thing, and I wasn't concentrating well. Having too much on my mind will make me run poorly. Lynn and Margaret had their heads in the race, while mine was still wandering over the terrain of sudden, unwelcome fame.

More than anything, I missed my close friends. When they heard how busy I was they backed off, saying they'd be around when I had time for them. One or two appeared to study me for signs of change after the Boston win, but I think I convinced them that I was as bewildered a celebrity as they would ever meet.

I got a boost by winning the Turkey Trot in Cape Elizabeth in November and beating some of the best local male runners. That carried me through to the last exam of my college career, in December. When it was over I went out for a long run. Moving along the snowy route to the ocean, I treasured one thought: now I could start to *think*. Now I had the freedom to see what came next.

SEVEN

*H*umorist Jean Shepherd tells of the advice he got from his grandfather upon reaching adulthood. I can't do Shepherd justice, but, to paraphrase, the advice was: "Don't wait for your life to start. It never starts." It may sound strange coming from me—the original goal setter—but I think Shepherd's grandfather was right. I don't let myself stagnate while I'm working on my goals. I try to experience life at the moment while looking toward the future.

I feel the same way as Jeff Drenth, a friend and teammate who died of unknown causes at the age of twenty-four. In his log, he wrote: "It is better to burn out than to rust." Jeff lived fully, and I try to copy his example. His friends from Athletics West ran together on the morning of Jeff's funeral, because we knew he would not want us to let his tragic death, a fluke that could have happened to anyone, make us afraid. Rather, we used it as an inspiration—each of us now bears part of the responsibility for keeping Jeff's spirit alive. We don't mean to be foolish in our activities, but neither will we stop taking some chances. We have to live.

There have been times when I've said "if only . . ." and

meant it. As I write, my major professional ambition is to run a sub-2:20 marathon. I tell myself I can stop competing so hard when that happens; I can get on with my life. But in my quieter moments I realize that life won't start with a sub-2:20 marathon. If I do beat that time there will be another goal to haunt me—maybe not a running ideal, but something. The trick is not to let the here and now suffer while the goal awaits. This is the perpetual tension of an athletic career.

As an athlete, you always have to wonder if you are allowing personal relationships to suffer while concentrating on your sport. I mentioned running away from Scott on a training loop. I had to hope that he would still be there when I returned, cramps and all. Another person might have been angry with me; he might have assumed that, in losing out to a training run, he'd seen how little he meant to me. I had to trust Scott to understand that love is love and running is running: there has to be room for both in my life or I won't be happy. I don't know what I would have done if Scott had asked me to choose between him and my sport, but fortunately he didn't.

We had one more test to put ourselves through before we were sure we wanted to spend our lives together. Nike offered me the chance to race and train in New Zealand in 1980—it was an opportunity to work on track events on the chance that I might qualify for the 1980 Olympics. Musicians dream of playing Carnegie Hall, mountain climbers aim to challenge K2, runners aspire to the Olympics. Despite Jacqueline Hansen's best efforts, a women's marathon wasn't sanctioned for the 1980 Games, so I figured I'd have to work on the 1,500 if I wanted to qualify for Moscow. There would be lots of high-quality runners in New Zealand, including Mary Decker, and I would be able to train in hot weather to prepare for summer in Moscow. But almost as soon as I arrived, the U.S. boycott was announced.

Scott still had a semester left at Bowdoin and wasn't thrilled to learn that I might not be in Maine with him. But he had plans of his own: after graduation he wanted to work long enough to earn his fare to Scandinavia, then travel there for a while. We knew we were in love, but we hadn't talked about marriage. I was up in the air as to what I'd do if my career didn't take off, so I couldn't tie Scott down. We parted in December with our future together very much in doubt. Both of us were free to pursue our goals, but I'm not sure either of us wanted to be in that position.

I went to New Zealand in January, making a few stops on the way. The first was in Oregon, where I visited Peter Leach and his family (no relation to Dr. Robert Leach). Peter was a pal from Bowdoin—if Scott had any competition over me, it was Peter. We went cross-country skiing on Mt. Hood in a snowstorm and I came down with weakness and chills, but I ascribed those to the altitude. Peter and I flew to San Francisco the next day; that evening I received the Best U.S. Female Distance Runner award from *Runner's World* at a banquet in Palo Alto. It was a great honor and made me forget about being sick. From there I flew to New Zealand.

I stayed on New Zealand's North Island with Ian Gamble and his family. Ian worked for Nike and often put runners up at his summer house near the beach. Driving from Auckland to his house I couldn't get over the number of sheep we saw grazing in the hills. They perched on inclined pastures at ridiculous angles—I got the feeling that one stiff breeze would bring them all down like so many rolling snowballs.

I had to run on those hills, but I never got used to them. It wasn't the altitude I minded, it was the energy drain of working on hills. I couldn't get a decent workout in the hot summer sun because so much of my strength was devoted to climbing the slopes.

The humidity was horrible. Maine usually has a short stretch of ninety-degree, humid weather every summer—when we get it, I always think of New Zealand. Running in it is like running with a soaking blanket wrapped around you. It's difficult to breathe, you perspire without feeling that you are losing any heat at all, and relief is rare. I developed a habit in New Zealand that I was happy to resume when I bought my house: I ran in the early morning, had a swim, ran in the late evening, and jumped into the ocean again. In Maine I have to plan my running around the tide table—I live on the edge of a clam flat that is flooded only at high tide, so I can't jump into the water anytime I feel like it. The result is the same, however—a few minutes' respite from the cloying air.

The New Zealand scenery was spectacular and the citizens were so far behind us that they were ahead of us. They aren't the sort of people who would pollute themselves half out of existence and then turn around and wonder what they had done. They are firmly dedicated to conservation of all natural resources.

But I didn't feel at home in other respects. Some runners like to travel to warm climates to train; I've never left Maine without wishing I didn't have to. I'm not at peace anywhere else, and, consequently, I don't train as well. Much as I liked the people and the environment, I knew I didn't want to stay in New Zealand for more than a few months. I had to get back on familiar ground in order to bring mind *and* body into condition.

I ran three races there. On January 19 I did the 1,500 in Christchurch, and felt I could perhaps hold my own in the shorter distances after all. On the twenty-sixth I ran the mile at Mt. Smart in Auckland; my time was 4:45, but the story that day was Mary Decker's world-record 4:21.7. Mary's success was inspiring; on February 3 I set a new American record at the Choysa Marathon in Auckland. The race began at six in the evening, but even so it was ninety-seven degrees. I kept thinking about Mary's amazing time as I pushed myself along the course; I came in at 2:31:23, then the second fastest women's marathon ever. Only Grete Waitz had run faster.

Two days later I came in from an easy run and swim and got into the shower. Soaping up the left side of my body I felt something strange under my arm. The area had been tender for some time, but I hadn't paid much attention to it. Runners always have aches and pains; if we stopped to examine every tender sensation we'd never train. I put the soap down and rinsed my fingers so I could probe more carefully. Playing the fingers gently over my skin, I felt a lump. It was the size of a plum, and it moved slightly, like a sack of gelatin, when I touched it.

I was frightened. Everyone thinks of cancer when she feels a lump under her skin. I immediately went to a doctor and he was reassuring. He said it was probably a clogged sweat gland that had become infected. The constant rubbing of my arm against my side had probably made the infection worse. That was plausible, but when the lump was no smaller four days later, despite careful attention from me, I decided to head back to Oregon. It was February 8; my "few months" in New Zealand were cut to one. As usual, I wanted to keep the news from my parents until I knew what was wrong, and I was sure Peter Leach would help me find a good doctor.

I planned to stay in Oregon for a while, but the visit was abbreviated on the advice of Peter's physician. He was so concerned about the lump that he wanted to admit me to the hospital right away for surgery. I balked at having the procedure done so far from home, however. Instead, I went to Maine and saw our family doctor. He referred me to a surgeon, who diagnosed the lump as a cystic hydroma. He said there was no hurry about operating because the lump was probably benign. He scheduled the surgery for March 31 so I could go to France with the U.S. Cross-Country team in the beginning of the month.

The trip to France turned out to be one I could have missed very happily. To begin with, I was exhausted from day one (I got into the spirit of things and wrote *Je suis très fatiguée* in my log). We arrived in Paris on March 3 and I spent much of the day sleeping. I figured I was suffering from jet lag. Over the next six days we kept a fairly easy schedule of running and sightseeing, though I had to miss a Picasso exhibit at the Louvre because it was up in a high cupola and I couldn't muster the energy to climb the stairs.

When in France to run, you run. On March 9 I came in twenty-sixth at the cross-country championships at Longchamps. All I could do was throw up my hands and accept my time, even though it was frustrating to be running so badly and not know why. None of the doctors had said that the lump would affect my running, so I couldn't blame that. I was eating well, sleeping nine or ten hours a day, and not pushing my training. I felt trapped inside a weakling body.

The day after Longchamps we went to Milan for the Cinque Milini cross-country race, but I was too tired to run. I thought that was the low moment of the trip. I was wrong.

The journey home was a nightmare. In Paris we sat on the apron for three hours while the crew tried to repair a malfunctioning instrument on the plane's control panel. Then we were fed lunch and sat a while longer. After five hours the repair attempt was abandoned and we were transferred to another plane; we took off half an hour later. There was turbulence over Newfoundland and Nova Scotia. A team of boxers had crashed in Poland while we were in France, and we couldn't help but think, "Here goes another athletic team in the middle of some nasty air." But the worst effects were some spilled drinks and airsickness. We made it to Kennedy late that night.

I raced to La Guardia Airport in a cab that must have been airborne a few times, only to find that my plane had been delayed two hours in Atlanta. By the time we took off for Portland, I was feeling very sick. I tried to sleep, hoping the queasiness would go away. I was awakened by an announcement from the pilot: it was too foggy to land in Portland, so we were going to Bangor.

If it hadn't been happening to me, I might have thought it was funny. Who had booked this trip, the Rod Serling Travel Agency? By the time I got my bags together in Bangor the only transportation left to Portland, two and a half hours away, was a school bus. I told the airline no thanks and rented a car with three other people, arriving in Portland at about two in the morning.

I was sick to my stomach all night, sicker than I'd been since I broke my leg. I had chills and a fever and couldn't run, so I did laundry all day because I was due to leave for the Shamrock Run in Florida the next morning. As bad as I felt, I wanted to go; I figured I could lie in the sun and rest. I may have been foolish, but I honestly believed that the trip to France had only upset my schedule and I wasn't actually sick. I hate to admit I'm sick.

I had no spunk running that week; I thought the heat was bothering me. Somehow, I summoned enough energy to win the Shamrock. Though the temperature the night before was eighty-five degrees, I had gone to bed wrapped in several blankets. Then I ran, and after the race I was chilled and thirsty. I had a pain in my side, as though I'd eaten something indigestible.

Like most people, I'm reluctant to see a doctor when I feel ill. Health may be the greatest asset of an athlete, but we're human—we're worried about what doctors will say. When you get sick you have to hand your life over to someone else for the duration. That can be a few days, a week, or longer. I can't stand doing that. Other people decide everything for a patient, and because I am a notoriously bad patient when it comes to following orders, I am watched very carefully. Casual friends call my house and ask if I'm taking it easy, prepared to deliver a lecture if I'm not. As a result, I long ago decided that my health had to be a secret from most people most of the time. So I let illness drag on until I can't function, then see a doctor. It isn't smart, but it's a habit I'm not likely to break.

Most distance runners guard information about their fitness the way I do, and it's easy, since there's no mecca where we all go to train and test ourselves against others. Men, especially, hate to give anything away to their opponents. If you watch a pre-race press conference, the men will be tight-lipped and speak only in platitudes ("I think I'm in pretty good shape"—this from a man who's about to shatter a world record); the women might reveal more, but not much. Ingrid Kristiansen is the most honest runner I know in this sense; before America's Marathon/Chicago in 1985 she said she was in terrific shape and hoped to break 2:20. Reporters asked me how I thought I'd do, and I said, "Ingrid's awfully tough" and "I hope to keep up with her." True statements, but they ducked the question. Actually, my training loops had been faster than ever and I was in the best shape of my life with the possible exception of 1984. But I wouldn't have revealed that unless electrodes had been applied to my fingertips. Runners like to save a whole lot of surprises for the race itself. The attitude is: You want to know what kind of shape I'm in? Then get in the race and see if you can keep up with me.

Any information I might give out about my fitness is a potential energy thief. I then have to run the race wondering what my competitors are thinking about. If I say I'm in great shape, they might find that statement an incentive to challenge me; I can see myself digging very deep to beat someone who said such a thing. In a sport like marathoning, you use every available inspiration—positive and negative—to keep going in a race. That doesn't mean you wish the other runners ill, but if one of them announces that she's in great shape, you're going to take advantage of it to pump yourself up. A race is as much a mental challenge as a physical one. That's the reason I don't like to eat dinner with my competition the night before a race. Judi St. Hilaire and Jacqueline Gareau are among my best friends, but I won't see them for a pre-race meal. Other runners sap your mental energy—you look at them and wonder what they're thinking and how they're feeling. I'll eat with race directors, coaches, family, and friends, but I can't cope with the strain of being with runners close to a big race. Perhaps I don't want them to see how nervous I get.

Anyway, the day after the Florida race I went to the beach in the afternoon and had a massage. When the masseuse worked my stomach muscles I almost hit the ceiling—it felt as if somebody were attacking from the inside with stilettos. Since I have a history of stomach upsets after races, I ignored this warning. I was afraid that a doctor would give me a lecture about staying on the beach too long and getting a bad sunburn. I explained my thirst and chills that way: sunburn can make you as sick as flu.

My hosts planned to take the visiting competitors to the greyhound racetrack that night. When I staggered in from my massage I told them to go ahead without me. As they were leaving, one turned and asked if I was sure they couldn't do something for me. "Well," I said, huddled on the couch and dripping sweat, "I guess I'd better see a doctor." The pain in my abdomen was worse than any I'd ever experienced. The stilettos had been exchanged for broadswords.

A doctor from the club examined me and arranged for transportation to the hospital. Nobody knew what was wrong, and I called my brother Andy to let him know where I was. He is a physician, so I thought he'd be able to answer my parents' questions better than I could. I was afraid I might be dying. Better for news like that to come from their son than from a stranger.

The club doctor turned me over to a surgeon, who sent in an anesthesiologist, who was followed by nurses and technicians. It took them the evening to discover the trouble. The news was good and bad—I had a hot appendix (this was the good news; I knew about appendicitis), but it was at the point of bursting (the bad news: if they didn't get to it in time I could be in for a long hospital visit). They hustled me into surgery the next morning and did get to the appendix in time. Apparently, the thing could have gone at any time during the Shamrock race, and I might well have died. I deserved the chewing out I got from the doctor for not heeding the early signs of distress.

In the hospital I read a *Sports Illustrated* article about Craig Virgin, who'd won the race at Longchamps. The writer called him a "big fish in a big pond." Extending that metaphor, the writer also mentioned that I had introduced the "barracuda" (in French, as he said, *"le grand poisson"*) to the U.S. team, which in turn introduced it to competing teams. A barracuda is an unexpected bite on the derrière, a sneak attack; it was something I'd picked up at Bowdoin. It's meant in fun, and I only mentioned it to the others because I thought it would relieve the tension of international competition. Everybody thought it was a riot. It was especially funny to hear someone with a foreign accent yell "Barracuda!" (in French it sounded like a pop love song) and then hear a yelp from the victim. *Sports Illustrated* mentioned that British runner Sebastian Coe was barracuda-ed in Paris.

But when I read the article I was thunderstruck. Maybe I was overreacting, but I couldn't help but worry. What would my parents think? What would my parents' friends say? I was afraid I would never persuade anyone that I wasn't a complete wild woman. The appendectomy must have driven the barracuda out of my parents' minds; they have never mentioned it.

I didn't escape without a reprimand, however. As the anesthesia began to wear off, I saw the surgeon by my bedside. When he was sure I was conscious, he said, "You know, sometimes we say things in the operating room that never leave that room. That barracuda should never have escaped your small circle of friends." Ever since then I have monitored my public behavior very carefully.

I've heard celebrities moaning about the difficulties of public life. In one way, I agree with them: my private life is nobody's business unless I choose to make it so. But I also think that it is critical to set good examples for the youth of this world.

I'm not a superwoman without human failings. But I try to live in such a way that no one will feel troubled about looking up to me. It's a way of giving something back to all the people who've supported my career by writing letters and cheering on the roadsides. The barracuda incident helped to clue me in to these responsibilities and I don't regret the lesson.

The day after I was released from the hospital in Florida I went running for fifteen minutes on the beach. The next day I did thirty minutes on a golf course. I only ran fourteen miles that week, and rode a stationary bicycle to get back in shape. Of course there was some discomfort, but I couldn't let my muscles go soft. I'm a believer in mind over matter: I can hover above sensations of pain if I think I'm doing my training some good. It is difficult to draw parallels between my activities as an athlete and those of someone in another profession, but perhaps a good analogy is to compare a side-lined athlete with a painter who has arthritis. Just as the artist will, if he is committed enough, take the brush in his teeth when his hands give up, so will some dedicated athletes undergo difficult training to keep in condition. Sometimes I don't have any choice: I can't slow down because the part of my brain that drives me won't allow it. There was no way to convince me that I should be resting completely while I waited for my surgery scars to heal.

I came back to Maine on April 10, a week after leaving the hospital. The next morning I ran ten miles before checking in to the Maine Medical Center for the cystic hydroma removal. The surgery was performed the following day and I don't remember much about it except that the surgeon told me the cyst was the size of an egg. I was home in three days.

Peter Leach came east to run in the Boston Marathon that week. I was planning to do radio commentary, but was too tired (and, maybe, disappointed that I couldn't race) to make the trip. Early in the afternoon I got a call from a high school friend who worked for the Associated Press. She wondered if I'd ever heard of a runner named Rosie Ruiz, who was the first woman to hit the tape.

"It's the weirdest thing, Joanie," she said. "She hardly looks sweaty, she's wearing a T-shirt instead of a singlet, and the colors she has on match the medal ribbon to a T."

I thought it must be a hoax, and so it was. Rosie Ruiz had covered most of the course via mass transit. I felt bad for Jacqueline Gareau, the real winner.

I didn't know Jacqueline then, but I wrote to her that evening. I didn't want her to miss the excitement of a win in Boston, so I told her what a great race I thought she'd run. She wrote back, one thing led to another, and now we are close friends.

You have to pick your friends in my sport, but there are many fine people involved. I've been lucky: Boston adopted me and the other New England runners and we've gotten to know each other there. The support system among women runners is phenomenal, but we're not above playing head games with each other. I sometimes run with Judi St. Hilaire, Lynn Jennings, and (in the summer) Jacqueline. We promise each other that our morning run will be an easy one because we want to get in a track workout during the afternoon, but as soon as we hit the road it's a race. Nobody wants to admit she is having a hard time. "You took the pace," one will say; "No, you took it" is the response. Finally, a couple of weeks later, we'll be talking to each other on the phone and one of us will mention the run. Casually, of course. "You remember that run we took? How fast were you going?" Then, before we hang up, we both admit we were sore for two days afterward.

Judi St. Hilaire reminds me of Julie Shea in one way: she loves to turn track workouts into races. I blame myself. I get her out onto the road and try to run her into the ground, so when we hit the track she shows no mercy. I can usually outlast her in the longer intervals, but I know what's coming. She'll promise not to run under seventy seconds for the last quarter and then run sixty-six; in the meantime, I'm panting along behind her wondering how I got into this mess. If we trained together every day we'd be whipped all the time.

The media and general public don't expect Judi and Jacqueline to beat me in road races. Sometimes I feel real tension between us over that fact. They don't have my experience, so they haven't yet equaled my achievements. There's tension on my side, too: I want both of them to do well, but I hate being beaten by either. When we are racing we have to be all business. If we didn't enjoy competition we wouldn't put on the numbers and enter races. But everyone who competes in a sport has to understand that it is serious. I'm trying to win on every level, as is everyone else. We can all pull for each other, but if we don't pull for ourselves first we'll soon be spectators.

Jacqueline's talent is something I haven't been able to gauge, but I know Judi has every bit as much ability as I do and maybe more. What Judi has lacked over the years and is beginning to gain is confidence. If she develops more of that she will be on her way. She zoomed past me in the 1985 L'eggs Mini on her way to one of the best finishes of her career. I finished way back and wasn't pleased, but I couldn't help but be delighted for Judi, even if it meant that she'd be much more competitive.

The other thing most runners understand and don't talk about is the fact that everything can blow up in your face without warning. I worried about the loss of my running career from the moment I realized I had one. On top of that, I sometimes wondered if it wasn't ridiculous for a grown woman to be running in circles. I've tried to develop backup plans in case something should happen to terminate my career. My first job after college was as a substitute teacher at Cape Elizabeth High, and it began in April.

I recovered from surgery quickly enough to run a 3,000m race at the Syracuse YMCA on April 26 and won in 9:50. The next day Frank Shorter and I teamed up for the Trevira Twosome in Central Park and were beaten by Herb Lindsay and Margaret Groos and Dick Quax and Anne Sullivan. Frank has been a friend over the years—once in a while he'll call just to see how I am. There's still a little starstruck voice inside me that says "Frank Shorter!" every time I see him, because I remember his amazing 1972 Olympic Marathon victory and all the gritty duels he ran with Bill Rodgers.

I was back in Portland and in bed early that night, since my job started in the morning. I taught for six weeks, and every morning I would rise at five in order to run before school. After teaching gym all day I'd run again. At night I literally collapsed. The students were playing softball at that time and I usually ended up as pitcher, expending more energy than they were.

I made a mistake teaching at Cape Elizabeth. Not only did I have trouble regarding my former teachers as colleagues, but I couldn't exert any authority on kids who knew me from the days when I hung out with their older brothers and sisters. Maybe if I had taught in a crowd of strangers I would have been better off. I couldn't open the door to the teachers' lounge without expecting to hear someone say, "What do you think you're doing in here?" It was also my first encounter with unmotivated students. Gym had always been one of my favorite classes, but I discovered that there were plenty of kids who didn't share my enthusiasm. They had to be all but dragged from the locker room to the gym—I would hear myself asking if they wanted me to call the principal and I'd cringe—and once there they refused to participate. I didn't know what to do. It's quite a shock for someone who's spent a lifetime regulating herself to encounter people who demand discipline.

My experience at Cape Elizabeth probably got me off to a bad start with the Boston University track team a year and a half later. I was helping to advise the distance runners, and was worried that they would show me as little respect as some of the Cape kids had. I stayed more distant than I would have liked during my first year at B.U. and maintained authority through mystery. Always highly self-motivated, I had trouble understanding that others needed coaching. I took reluctance to train as an insult to my authority, when it should have been clear that some runners need to be prodded into reaching their best potential. It isn't weakness on their part—it's a different motivational style.

The six weeks at Cape High passed slowly. I ran races almost every weekend to keep in shape and to remind myself that there were plenty of people in the world who loved to run. I had a strict daily schedule to manage the demands of teaching, so my training didn't suffer much. I won the Charlie's Surplus race in Worcester, Massachusetts, in mid-May and had a personal best—55:12 for ten miles. That proved I could hang in there with a full-time job. Even so, it was a relief to finish teaching in early June; I drew a smiley face in my log next to the notation that this was my last day at school.

In late May I attended commencement exercises and officially graduated from Bowdoin, then said a hurried good-bye to Scott before he left for home. We'd been seeing each other again while I was living with my parents, and I think we were both convinced that the relationship was going someplace. He still had his dream of a year in Scandinavia, however, and I couldn't ask him not to go. Our parting at graduation wasn't too heart-wrenching: he was going to spend the summer working and getting his pilot's license in Wiscasset, Maine, an easy distance from Cape Elizabeth.

Once I had a bit of free time I realized I was tired. The Worcester race happened to start almost at the doorstep of a chiropractor named Ken Harling, whom I'd been encouraged to see by a sports physiologist I knew in Maine. I went to his office several times in the next few months for spinal adjustments. I was not convinced that the treatment did any good, but since I used to borrow my mother's VW beetle to bump down to Worcester and back, I don't see how I can judge the results fairly. I kept at it because of the fatigue. Dr. Harling told me it looked as if I were only running on one leg, so to speak. If his treatments could help me spread the strain more evenly through my body, I was all for them.

Submitting to chiropractic medicine was a significant change for me. I used to look upon runners who underwent regular massage therapy and other training "luxuries" and think, "You need that junk? I can beat you without any of it." I admit I expressed this attitude to fire myself up when I was scared of the opposition, but it was childish nonetheless. I now work with a masseuse and a physical therapist, and through the years I have tried many different treatments to alleviate soreness, fatigue, and lack of mobility. I would have considered physical therapy a luxury not long ago. Now I know it is a necessity, particularly for top-level athletes. We abuse our bodies and we need skilled people to help us put ourselves back in order.

When I went to Dr. Harling, I was beginning to recognize that there were many ways to help myself. I knew that even if he did my body no good, he was doing something for my mind. Driving back and forth to Worcester was a chore, but by doing so I had reaffirmed my decision to be a real athlete. There are any number of opportunities to quit a sport like running—because of family pressure, excessive injury, having your life taken over by training, experiencing a down year, whatever—so the athlete has to seek out ways to affirm the original commitment. My trips to Worcester were ratifications. I was becoming a real runner, learning to use everything at my disposal to make myself better. With time and experience I would be able to judge which extra-athletic therapies were helpful and which weren't.

These things take time, though, and 1980 and 1981 were building years for my career. My results through the spring and summer of 1980 were mixed. In the beginning of June I broke Patti Lyons's record in the Litchfield Road Race; at the end of the month I came in fourth in the Cascade Runoff in Oregon.

Of course I tried to analyze what I was doing wrong. My schedule was full of professional and personal duties; as soon as I left teaching and had some free time I packed it with things to do. I didn't try to take a normal job that summer, but, even so, I was busy. Since the U.S. wasn't going to the Olympics, I might have slowed down my training, but instead I switched back to concentrating on the longer distances I preferred. My philosophy has always been, "When in doubt, run harder." Besides, physical fatigue never gets me down. I have what sometimes seem to be limitless sources of energy. What does get me down is mental fatigue—being pulled this way and that, being unable to concentrate on my work. I didn't know how to fight that, so I kept wearing myself down even further.

There were all kinds of warnings that I should reorganize my priorities: fourth place at the Avon Marathon in London, fourth in Falmouth, second to Laurie Binder in a half-marathon in Oregon, the list goes on. I had some encouraging results, but not enough to make me happy. I was running over a hundred miles a week, so I knew the problem wasn't totally physical. I was at a loss.

Because I was having such a tough time, I felt slightly out of place at the Association of Road Racing Athletes (ARRA) meeting in Chicago in September. I was wondering if I was washed up even as I discussed the topic of the day: amateurism vs. professionalism. There are always athletes who show remarkable promise and then fade away; I couldn't keep from wondering if I was one of those.

But I went to the meeting and voiced my opinions. The meeting triggered a series of events that lead to the Cascade Runoff's awarding prize money for the first time in June 1981. The Athletic Congress (TAC), which had succeeded the AAU as running's governing body, declared those athletes who accepted prize money to be professional, and therefore ineligible to compete in amateur races. With the backing of the ARRA, the athletes in question went on competing anyway. We met later in 1981 to stand by that decision and to take it one step further. Some athletes were hogging all of the available money through exorbitant clinic or consulting fees. To put an end to that practice, the ARRA voted that race sponsors should provide prize money to a certain number of finishers of each sex (sometimes the money extends as far as twentieth place); anything left over from these payments could go for consulting fees if the sponsor wished to pay them. This measure has helped innumerable runners who can't command such clinic fees.

TAC went along with our decision after a lot of pressure was applied. But it didn't like the idea of the sport going professional in all but the technical sense, so it set up trust funds for runners. All prize money goes into these funds. Athletes may draw upon them for normal training expenses (equipment, travel, medical, etc.), but the balance stays in their accounts until they stop competing. On the other hand, clinic fees are not diverted—anyone who can earn them can keep them. It's a compromise that satisfied the ARRA and TAC.

My worry is that young runners coming out of college will run for the money and do themselves harm. I've been running for a good while and I'm still waiting for the quality class of rookies that should have been challenging me by now. Several runners may have burned themselves out in pursuit of the big bucks. Those coming up should realize that, though running is extremely popular and much more lucrative than it once was, it's not something to pursue for the money. Even the top runners are paupers compared to their counterparts in golf, tennis, and the major team sports. I voted for the inclusion of prize money in races because I was working hard and believed I deserved compensation; but more than that, I had the feeling (after a few years of trying to train and hold down other jobs) I wasn't going to get where I wanted to go unless I could treat running as a full-time job. Money was a tool, not a goal.

Because I haven't had to pursue another career, I'm able to include the extras in my training program where amateurs of other times couldn't. It's the second run of the day that makes me the competitor I am. I run very hard in the morning, every morning, so in the afternoon I'm tired. That's when I push myself to give more than I think I can. The benefits are tremendous: this workout teaches me my limits, shows me how much heart I have, and brings my mental stamina up to its highest level. I couldn't face an afternoon run if I had to work eight or nine hours a day at a job—it's too challenging, too consuming. So I'm grateful to get money for what I do. But it's good that I didn't expect it when I started out. I run because I love to—that's the way it's been from the beginning. If I stopped loving it I'd quit without a thought about the money. I hope the young runners of today feel that way—they'll need to if they want long careers. I can't imagine going through the agony of injuries and down years with only monetary goals in mind. You have to pursue excellence for a more meaningful reason.

The same principle applies to the fact that I usually won't commit to a race too far in advance. Race directors may think I'm being coy when I can't be sure in June that I'll be fit to run a race in October. I understand their problems; they need to publicize my participation early because I might attract spectators or other prominent runners to a race. Often the organizers will dangle a great deal of money before me, saying, in effect, "We don't mind if you don't run well. Just promise you'll be there and you can do what you like." Well, I can't function that way. I will not put myself on a starting line unless I know I'm up to a race, except when I have already committed. No amount of money can compensate me for selling myself out. It's a matter of pride, but pride isn't always a bad thing. I've held on to my dignity and, I hope, my integrity; the needling from reporters and race directors is something I can live with as long as I can keep liking myself. When a reporter suggests that I'm holding out for more money or a race organizer calls and says I'm messing up his life, I get momentary urges to retire. I care what reporters and promoters think, but I can't let them get to me. If I haven't earned their respect with consistency and fair dealing, so be it.

Throughout my career I've made adjustments to preserve my self-respect. Nowadays that involves training hard and racing when I'm ready. In 1980, I was losing self-respect because I was neither achieving success nor working toward a more stable career. As I said before, part of my reason for teaching was that I saw it as a possible safety net. For the same reason, when Nike offered me a job in its sports research lab in Exeter, New Hampshire, I took it. I wasn't ready to make running a full-time job and I still had a nagging voice inside saying, "Running in circles isn't enough. You must have a real job as well." I felt more secure with a lot of options.

I moved to Exeter in November. I couldn't have asked for more sympathetic employers; it was understood that I was always free to take off for a race. So I didn't have a fixed position at the lab—I moved around and worked where I was needed. Because I moved around so much, working on everything from oxygen intake and utilization tests to stress tests for shoes, I didn't feel I was making much of a contribution. The best thing I could do for Nike was to improve my racing results, and that wasn't happening. And while I was in New Hampshire I trained with the men who also ran and worked for Nike. It was a big mistake. They were much better runners; I was training under racing conditions instead of building myself up at my own pace.

In 1981, when Patti Lyons Catalano was dominating the sport, the year started well for me. Greg Meyer and I traveled the Anheuser-Busch Natural Light Half-Marathon circuit as co-hosts. I won in New Orleans in January, setting a new American best of 1:13.26, and again in San Diego with another record of 1:11.16 in March. After the New Orleans race I wrote in my log, "What a good feeling to finally have again." But shortly after San Diego I felt tired and draggy again. The record didn't mean as much to me in March because I thought I should be running even faster. Something was wrong and I couldn't pinpoint it.

From then on the year belonged to Patti. She beat me in Jacksonville, Florida, in New Orleans, in Litchfield, Connecticut, and in New York City. Our rivalry (if you could call it that) was interrupted by the Boston Marathon. Patti was overtaken by Allison Roe, but she came in second while I had to settle for third.

It was discouraging to run third in Boston, but I might have done worse. I had met David Hemery, the track coach at Boston University, by then and discussed the prospect of helping out with B.U.'s distance runners. In the middle of the marathon, when I was running poorly enough to finish in the second ten, I thought, "Hey, those coaches and athletes from B.U. are watching. If you want the experience of helping college athletes, shape up." That helped me gain a respectable time.

I really can't explain my disappointing finish in Boston. It wasn't the place so much as the sluggishness I felt throughout the race. The field was very competitive that year, perhaps the most competitive it has ever been. I had high hopes of winning for a second time, but they were quickly dampened when I found myself as far back as eleventh in the first half of the race. Allison and Patti were in a class by themselves that day. I knew they were forces to be reckoned with, but I didn't expect so many other runners to show me their backsides in the early stages. My biggest asset, my fluid stride, abandoned me that day.

I was getting somewhat depressed, because I couldn't figure out what was wrong. Instead of examining the differences in my life-style from the 1979 Boston win on, I pushed ahead and tried to force myself to run better. I should have realized that I wasn't taking good care of myself. I was involved in too many activities that had nothing to do with running, I was traveling too much, and I wasn't eating correctly. There was no time (so I thought) to prepare balanced meals. All the indications were that I should straighten out my priorities, but it was as if I were being tumbled in a wave—I thought I had no choice but to go along with it. The lesson didn't take for years.

I might have changed my ways if my results had been consistently awful, but they weren't. I had good races now and then, enough to postpone any meaningful inquiries into my problems. I set an American record (1:26.10) for 25k at the Old Kent River Bank run in Michigan, felt I'd licked the snags, then ran a poor seventh in the L'eggs Mini a few days later. And so it went through the summer.

Probably the most difficult race was the TAC National 10,000m finals in Sacramento. The temperature was ninety-four degrees, and there were no provisions made for us to take water or run through spray, so we sweltered. I took the lead after two laps and held it to the end, winning in a time of 33:37.5. But in the evening the soreness in my heels returned; since I had just run a hard race in spikes, it was worse than ever. For the next couple of weeks I swam and rode a bicycle so as to remove the pressure from my feet. By the first week of July I was running over ten miles a day again, even though the heels continued to give me some trouble. I won the Natural Light race on Cape Cod later that month and the discomfort got worse. But I pushed myself to run over ninety miles a week because I was preparing for Falmouth.

In the meantime I told David Hemery that I would appreciate the experience of helping him at B.U. and went to Boston for orientation in July. I left Exeter in mid-June to train in Maine and prepare myself for my new responsibilities. However, I decided to keep my apartment in Exeter for the summer, as I made frequent visits there for testing and shoes. The day before the Falmouth race, I borrowed Dad's station wagon and took a load of stuff from Exeter to Boston. On the way I picked up Scott at the Boston Greyhound bus station—he was coming in from Alaska.

Scott hadn't made it to Scandinavia. After his summer in Maine he worked at a ski resort in Colorado. From there he went to California, where he had a bouncer job, fried hamburgers at a Jack in the Box, and sold fishing magazines over the phone. He then signed on with an Alaskan fishing boat.

Finally I couldn't stand it anymore—I missed him. We corresponded while he drifted from here to there; his letters said how much he cared, but his westward travels made me wonder. When he came off the boat there was a letter from me saying, "Are you *ever* coming back? Please come back!"

So he did. No one has ever looked better to me: I can still see him in that grimy bus terminal, sunburned, googly-eyed from culture shock. He has a one-of-a-kind smile—one look at that put my doubts about our relationship to rest. We went to Falmouth, where, maybe on love, I ran 38:15.5 and came in first.

On August 23 I ran the Avon International Marathon in Ottawa. It was horrible. My time was 2:37:24 and I wrote in my journal, "Hot, poison ivy, and pit stop pretty much sums it up for a bad experience." It's the only time I can remember making a pit stop in a race. I like to know the location of all the portable toilets on a course, just in case, but I don't expect to have to stop. And it was tough to run with poison ivy. I was sweating more than usual because of the high humidity, and when the moisture hit the rash, the itchiness was almost unbearable.

My late summer racing schedule and my new responsibilities with the distance runners at B.U. caught up with me in the fall. I averaged only eighty training miles a week in October and November, and each mile was a struggle. I noticed that the clerical staff at B.U. was better able to climb stairs than I was. Some of them smoked, but I was the one panting for breath after a few flights. I remembered my siege at N.C. State and hoped I wasn't coming down with mono again.

Over Thanksgiving I discussed the problem with my brother Andy at his house in Boothbay Harbor. I told him how tired I felt, so we went to his hospital, where he tested my blood. I was anemic. My hemoglobin count was 9.8; the normal range for a woman is between 12 and 14. Andy said that was clearly part of the cause of my exhaustion, along with my demanding schedule. For once the problem *was* physical, and it was getting me down. It was an exception to the rule that I normally suffer from mental, not physical, exhaustion.

Between my bothersome heels (which had been affecting the consistency of my training for some time) and my fatigue, I was ready for drastic measures—I decided that it was time to go through with heel surgery. Bob Sevene, who was coaching the B.U. male distance runners and helping me with my training, had been suggesting the procedure since the Nationals in Sacramento. Both he and Dr. Leach were optimistic that the operation would help me. Initially, the surgery was scheduled for November, but Doc Leach refused to operate until I overcame the anemia, which I did with adjustments to my diet. We rescheduled for late December.

Early in December I was committed to the Natural Light final at Busch Gardens in Florida. I had agreed to run when

I signed on as co-host of the series. Cathy Twoomey beat me by a full minute. I wrote: "There wasn't anything I could do about it. Too wiped to jog afterwards." It was awful to want to move and to be held back by a body that wouldn't cooperate. I kept signaling for more energy from my legs, but there wasn't anything they could do either.

I sometimes think athletes and newly disabled people have much in common. I imagine disabled people waking up in the morning and taking inventory of their capacity for physical activity that day: "How are my legs working? Can I stand the pain today? Should I make plans or should I lie here a while longer?" The amazing thing is that those men and women, especially the ones with unpredictable diseases like multiple sclerosis, are able to rise above their bodies so frequently. They do things that appear impossible. An athlete makes the same sort of survey every day when things aren't going right. I had to talk myself into running every morning. I was tight and tired after the Tampa race—I ran only thirty-eight miles that whole week. The next week, only twenty miles. There was now no question in my mind that surgery was the logical course of action to take for my heel problems. Walking was beginning to be a real challenge.

Dr. Leach removed bone spurs and scar tissue from both heels in December. My right Achilles tendon was partially torn, so he repaired that. He also removed both bursa sacs, which had ruptured. What he didn't do was give me a lecture or display me to young runners as I lay in bed with my two casts. I was grateful.

Before I left the hospital I was given walking casts. That was a mistake: Susan Hughes, a close friend and something of a surrogate mother, picked me up at the hospital on New Year's Eve and took me to her house in Needham, where I tried to dance in the light casts that night. The next morning

I drove my car—a challenge—but that evening Scott was behind the wheel on our return to Maine.

Scott and I are famously woolly drivers. We're always late, always in a hurry. But that night, we started out with a clear sense of caution. It was pouring rain. The rain changed to snow at the Maine Turnpike entrance in Kittery and the driving was terrible. We had a minor accident near our exit, but no one was hurt.

It was an ominous beginning to 1982. I was starting the new year almost overwhelmed with doubts. I'd had nothing to lose by undergoing surgery, since the heels would have terminated my career if unrepaired, but I wasn't sure I'd gained anything either. Only my faith in Dr. Leach kept me from believing I would never run competitively again.

EIGHT

A scary thing happened before I had surgery: I "hit the wall" at the Columbus Bank One Marathon in early November. The muscles in my legs ran short of glycogen (their fuel) late in the race, and, despite a second-place finish, I hobbled to the line in 2:39:07, behind Charlotte Teske of West Germany. I had no business being there; I was anemic and my heels were in terrible shape. But I didn't know about the anemia, and I figured it was better to cope with the soreness than stop running. Having my body turn traitor was a surprise. I was moving along—feeling sluggish, yes, but not too bad—when there was this terrible, unfamiliar sensation in my legs. I had no choice but to slow down. My legs kept cramping and losing steam, but before they were completely used up I saw the finish line—that was enough to bring me across. I drank a quart of water and felt better.

That experience taught me a lesson. Two lessons, in fact: you cannot go into a marathon unprepared, and anything can happen in such a long race.

The second lesson is one you learn at your peril, because once you're afraid of the marathon you have to develop ways of channeling the fear. I feel about marathons the way my parents taught me to feel about the ocean: it is a mighty thing and very beautiful, but don't underestimate its capacity to hurt you. This is what makes the marathon an exciting race for runners and spectators alike. The fans know we are pitting our relatively frail bodies against faster and faster times; and if anybody needs to be reminded of the danger involved, think of Gabriela Andersen-Schiess's alarming entrance into the Los Angeles Coliseum in August 1984. Limping around the track, bent double, she was obviously disoriented and dehydrated, but her condition could have been much worse. Marathoners are in better shape today than ever, but even seasoned runners must stay wary, or what happened to Gabriela could happen to them. It is even possible to suffer brain damage by running without proper conditioning. Still, if you become afraid of competition, that's the end; your concentration will suffer irreparably from fear. If you can take your concern and make it work for you, then it's a useful training tool. Gabriela is still competing, but her experience in Los Angeles made her wiser—she knows she shouldn't have run at that level in the heat, and now she is leery of hot days.

After hitting the wall I had new respect for the distance. With each subsequent marathon I've refined my training program a bit more. I start preparing three or four months in advance by taking one twenty-mile run per week. I cover about a hundred and twenty miles a week whenever I'm healthy—not many women run that much. So far, my results have been good; I've had a lot of injuries, but I've also had my share of fast races. I don't think I could give up those miles even as an experiment. Mileage is my safety blanket; I feel I'm doing okay if I can put in enough miles. My mental condition, how I feel about my training, is as important as my physical endurance. If you have confidence in your training it will show in your races.

I run before breakfast, and when I get home I cool down with a bowl of cereal and some fruit or juice. I don't do a lot of stretching; I start running slowly in order to warm up, and I get the kinks out at the end by pacing around the kitchen. Usually the telephone rings, so any attempt I make to stretch is interrupted. Until recently, the only time I stretched was before a race, when I have to get out of the gate quickly—not only because I don't sprint well at the end of a race, but because I can hear the pounding of running shoes behind me.

As a marathon nears I increase my training intensity. I run twenty miles once every five days, and on the other four I do a minimum of ten miles in the morning and six in the afternoon. It might seem logical to test myself with a twenty-six-mile run at least once a week, but I don't do that because I'm afraid it would wear me down, both physically and mentally. I know I should be able to run that distance in two hours and fifty minutes any day of the week. But suppose I had an off day and couldn't keep that pace? Then I would push myself to get faster and faster, sacrificing the storehouse of energy I need for the race. My training revolves around the time it takes me to do certain loops. I never cheat on mileage or cut corners. Some people who have run with me say I run farther than I admit, because I always take the longest possible route around a curve. My six-mile afternoon loop is probably closer to seven, but I won't measure it. My fastest time on that course is thirty-seven minutes, whereas my fastest 10k—6.2 miles—is 31:49, so it's obvious that I am running farther than I think. These days, as I try to break through to faster race times, I add even more distance to the loop by running farther and farther before turning back toward home. But I still like to call it six miles. If I get tired near the end I say to myself, "Come on, can't you go a measly six miles?" If I had to say "seven miles" I might not have the same incentive. I've learned to play tricks on myself.

If I feel good for nine straight days I run hard for nine straight days. I don't pencil in any easy days—they just happen, when my body won't cooperate. I always run the way I feel. I prefer to wake up in the morning knowing exactly how far I will run that day, so I go to bed with a firm notion in mind. I won't ask for something I can't deliver—like a twenty-mile run on a down day—because that would harm me mentally, and possibly physically. If I go out on a twenty-mile loop accepting the idea beforehand that I'm tired and may have to run fifteen, that's okay. But once I've decided how much I can accomplish, I won't do less under any but extraordinary circumstances. I may run more than I planned, but seldom less.

During 1985–86, when I was recovering from my second heel surgery, I added swimming to my schedule in such a significant way that I doubt I'll be able to do without it. It's a great exercise and I depend on it to take the edge off my high energy levels. But it's so boring! People say running is dull, but swimming makes roadwork seem like double overtime basketball. I get excited if I see a pin or something on the bottom of the pool—I look forward to it on the next lap. But I like what swimming does for me.

There are all sorts of ways to pass the time when I'm running. The scenery changes every day, even on my most familiar loops; I watch the progress of the seasons in the colors of grass and trees; I note the additions of baby cows and chickens on nearby farms; I welcome the great blue herons to the cove; and I try to run in the first snowstorm. I can also go inside my head and write a letter or try to remember the words to a song. When I'm looking for extra energy I'll pick out a tree down the road and try to get to it before a car passes me, or I'll pretend it's an opponent I have to catch.

As I've said, I enjoy running in Freeport because there are so few cars on my loops. When I hit the roads in Boston I have to concentrate on the traffic, which detracts from the workout. Once in a while a car will play chicken with me, heading straight for me and not veering away until I move. I'm usually so far into my concentration that I don't notice the car at first, and when I do see it I expect it to get out of my way—I never believe people are aiming for me. It's one thing for drivers not to realize that they are coming too close, but when they make a game of almost hitting me it's terrifying. I've always been bold enough to expect drivers to give me part of the road, and have had good luck with most. But even when I don't have to worry about a crazy, running in traffic is tough. I hate stopping for lights, leaping up onto a sidewalk and back down again when a car passes, and trying to pay attention to so many stimuli. In Freeport I can float along in whatever mental condition I choose—the only time I'm faked out is when two cars come from behind at once; I move over for the first, not realizing there's another behind, and get a scare when I lean back toward the center of the road.

I don't want to give the impression that I search for thoughts while training. Ideas present themselves and I think about them; then they drift away. If you took a car trip without a radio, you would rely on your brain to pass the time, but you wouldn't necessarily think momentous thoughts. Most of the time I'm not thinking about anything special. My mind goes off, I zone out, and when I'm finished running I come back to earth. All I know is that I'm never bored.

That's what my roadwork is like, day after day. While preparing for a marathon I probably do more testing on my long run. Very recently I have begun to worry about pacing myself in workouts. I used to run without thinking too much about split times—I knew I should run ten miles within a certain time limit to prove I was fit, but I didn't look at my watch during a workout; now I consciously try to run segments faster and faster as the big races approach. If, say, I can run the afternoon six-miler in forty-two minutes, I'll push to do it in forty the next day. I worry I won't keep up with some of my rivals if I don't include more time limits in my schedule. Some of them have endurance *and* speed, and every year they whittle away at my endurance advantage. I have to try to neutralize their speed.

The week before a marathon I taper off only slightly, if at all. I run at least eighty miles because I don't want my body to relax; I'm afraid the marathon will be a shock if I cut down too much. I feel geared up and need little sleep. Scott takes care of me for a couple of days before the race because I can't stay focused on details. He will remember to pack my extra shoes, choose the restaurants, deal with cab drivers, and tell me if it's chilly enough for a sweater.

My diet remains consistent at this stage. As the old joke goes, I'm on a "see food" diet: I see food and I eat it. I don't believe in carbohydrate loading or any other special regimen. My body is accustomed to certain foods and I don't want to hand it a surprise that close to a race. High carbohydrate diets may help some runners avoid hitting the wall, but for me, prime conditioning and a consistently good diet are a better prescription.

I don't rely on special foods or liquids. They can become crutches, and if a crutch gets kicked out from under a person, there is bound to be a big fall. If you depend on a particular food, what will you do when it isn't available? If you think you need a special solution to drink in a race, what happens if you can't work your way through the pack at the water station to get your bottle? Some runners have done remarkably well despite such requirements, but others have psyched themselves out of meaningful competition by becoming fanatics about food. I've always depended on my training and let the details take care of themselves.

My training for 10k racing is similar to my marathon preparation, except I try to run on a track more often to develop speed. One of the reasons Ingrid Kristiansen is the greatest 10k runner in history is that she got her start on the track; she can pour on the speed at the end of that distance.

The other big difference between marathon and 10k preparation is, for a marathon, I have to get ready for a letdown. The 10k doesn't require three or four months of intense work. Once I've run a marathon I immediately try to look ahead to the next race in order to keep away the feeling of emptiness, but it doesn't usually work. I've had the date of the race in my head for so long that once it's passed, I am lost for a time. I'm okay physically—a little sore but anxious to run in the ensuing week. The letdown is mental, and it hits about two weeks after the race. I become lethargic; I have to force myself to run loops in reasonable times. Because I know this low period is part of my pattern, I like to run only two marathons a year. Even that is stretching things; I ran three between April 1983 and August 1984 and was unable to attempt another until October 1985. I had all the energy in the world, but my brain wasn't up to snuff.

My routines may not be right for anyone else—in fact, they probably aren't, since I developed them under some unique circumstances. I've made advances by trying to beat injuries. After my heel surgery, for instance, I went to work on a stationary bicycle for lack of anything better to do. At first I rode fifteen or twenty minutes a day, and eventually increased the workout to forty-five minutes of warm-ups followed by a series of intervals: I would pedal hard for two minutes, then slowly for a minute, and so on. The object was to raise my heart rate. But because I couldn't run or just sit around, I found out how great a bicycle can be for cardiovascular fitness. I used that knowledge again in 1984, applying it to swimming, while trying to recover from arthroscopic knee surgery. I file away everything that works, because I know I'll use it again sometime.

Where I had let my problems get to me the year before, I went into 1982 with a new attitude: either my feet wouldn't heal properly and I'd have to stop running or they would be fine and I could do what I liked. Either way, I thought I could cope. My life would be different without competitive running, but I could look forward to a new beginning in another career. I had Scott, my family, my friends, and myriad interests to keep me plugging along.

With that clear in my mind, I started running again. The casts were removed in late January, and on February 20 I ran six miles in Cape Elizabeth; I'd done some jogging around the B.U. indoor track, but this was my first significant run after surgery. I had to coax myself into every step, but I anticipated soreness. What I hoped I wouldn't feel were tearing sensations, and I didn't. By the end of March I was running eighty miles a week, and I knew I was going to recover.

I took several B.U. qualifiers to the AIAW Nationals at the University of Northern Iowa on March 10. My biggest problem at B.U. occurred during this meet.

I entered Julie White in the pentathlon and the high jump. When I checked the entries, I saw she had been listed for the pentathlon but omitted from the high jump. I protested, but the officials said I had failed to enter her correctly. I showed them a carbon copy of the form, proving I did everything as directed, but Julie still wasn't allowed to compete. I don't know what I did wrong. Julie assured me that she was too exhausted from the pentathlon to be competitive in the high jump. I felt I should have found another way to fix things, and that I had robbed her of an opportunity. I still wonder what I might have done differently and how Julie would have fared in the jump. It doesn't seem so terrible now, but I brood about it.

That first year was rough for the team and me. What I did in Iowa made me question how much good I was doing them; I was still learning how to deal with athletes, but at least they should have been able to rely on my meet experience to make sure they were signed up for the correct events. I was too hard on myself and I took it out on them by not being as sympathetic to their needs as I might have been: I wanted them to do as I did, not as I said.

But we had our good times. All of us hated to run in the city because of the dirty air, noise, and cars, so I would take them to the outskirts of Brookline or Weston to run on dirt trails and quiet roads. Weston had a reservoir where we could lope around in peace. Because there were so many teams that took precedence over us, I wasn't always able to get a university van, so I would pile eight or nine people into my compact station wagon. One day, driving through the center of Brookline, we were pulled over by a policeman.

"This vehicle is overloaded," he said.

I couldn't argue with him. He made three or four runners get out of the car, and I told them, in his hearing, that they'd have to run the few miles home. It was rush hour and they'd have a struggle, but they agreed. I didn't get a ticket, but the policeman said if he caught me again he'd cite me. He watched the girls jog away before he left. When he was out of sight I drove around the block and picked them up on the other side.

Brookline was the scene of another encounter with the law. Marty Shea (not to be confused with Mary Shea, whom I trained with in North Carolina) liked to run in the morning because she had labs in the afternoon. I would drive her out to Brookline so she could run on the golf courses. One morning I heard a familiar sound and saw the blue lights flashing in the rearview mirror. The policeman accused me of speeding. He said he'd clocked me at twenty-five in a fifteen mile per hour zone. I said, "You've got to be kidding! I can run faster than I was driving." He let me off.

While I worked with the team, I was also keeping up with my own career. On April 19 Randy Thomas and I broadcast the Boston Marathon on WCVB. Much as I enjoyed the program, I missed being on the course as a competitor. But watching my favorite race may have given me the boost I needed, because after that my training picked up; I was methodically aiming at faster and faster practice runs. By May 8 I was in shape for my first race, the Old Kent River Bank Run, a 25k. I won in 1:26:30, taking ten seconds off my American record time. I knew I was well and back in form.

I can't explain my quick recovery from surgery. I didn't think I'd have a good running year in 1982, but it turned out to be one of my best. Maybe it was because I had put my mind to rest. But my overriding emotion was hope. I knew I could come back. Everything else was speculation from people who didn't live inside my body.

On Memorial Day I finished second in the L'eggs Mini behind Grete Waitz. I haven't won that race yet, but taking second place was very satisfying, especially since I ran what at that time was a personal best of 32:35.

In June I was a disheartening twelfth in the 5,000m in Oslo. This was my first taste of the European track circuit; I was overwhelmed by all of the new talent—new to me, anyway. I also went out too fast, running the first mile in 4:49. It was a disappointing race and a good lesson.

I redeemed myself with a 4:24.8 for 1,500m in Bergen. I was fourth, but by rights the 1,500 should have been too short for me, so I couldn't help but be pleased. Back in Oslo on July 3 I was second to Grete Waitz in a half-marathon by a minute and change. I had her in sight most of the way, which was all I'd hoped for.

I ran another 10k in Middletown, New York, on July 18, winning in 33:17. Diane Rogers was second, and Patti Lyons Catalano, having a down year after 1981, came in fourth. Patti is, I think, a classic example of someone who let her enthusiasm for running cloud her better judgment. She's been trying to come back since 1981 and had a good showing at the Olympic Marathon trials in 1984, but my feeling is that she hurt herself mentally and physically by running too much too soon. It's a shame—she had loads of talent and used to bubble about the sport even before she competed with us. Hers should have been a magical success story: a bright young woman takes up running to lose weight and ease the tension of quitting smoking, then goes on to the world-class ranks. But she couldn't maintain the effort, the underpinnings simply weren't there. She was smart to take a couple of years away from the sport in the early eighties to assess herself. Running has taken on new meaning for her now, and I hope she will be able to revive her career.

At the end of July I won a five-mile race in Portland, and two weeks later I set a new course record in the Falmouth

Road Race. My running summer ended with the Bobby Crim Ten Mile Road Race in Flint, Michigan, where I broke Patti's American record with 53:18.

I had helped with recruiting at B.U. in the spring and was looking forward to the new year. The team had acquired a certain fire over the summer, which made me feel more comfortable as its adviser. We were destined to inspire one another for the remainder of our time together. When my feet were healing I'd watched the runners' progress and tried to keep up with them; now that my running was going so well, they seemed to look to me for the mental juice to make them winners.

Boston University had only one woman earn All-American honors that season, a freshman named Barbara Higgins. She ran in a historic meet at the Pontiac Silverdome March 12. She was B.U.'s only NCAA qualifier, placing sixth in the 1,000-yard run. What made the event significant was that men and women were competing in the same place at the same time. The two sexes alternated events and that made for a more interesting meet. Women had been agitating for inclusion in the NCAA for a long time. They were now accorded equal travel allowances and other benefits, not the least of which was adequate press coverage.

My efforts at B.U. were finally showing some results, so before I traveled anywhere to race, I had to decide whether I could leave the team. If the answer was no, that was that. But sometimes I maneuvered myself into a yes; I learned to play the airline schedules for everything I could get.

I wanted to run in Oregon in early September at the Nike/Oregon Track Club Marathon. It had been almost a year since the Bank One race, so it was time to face up to the possibility of hitting the wall again. I knew I was in terrific shape—my blood count was good, my heels were cooperating, and my race results were hopeful—but this was my first marathon test since Columbus.

I could have run a different marathon that fall, but the Nike/OTC took place in Eugene, another of my backyards. I felt completely comfortable running there. My Nike friends lined the route along with the country's most knowledgeable spectators. All the citizens of Eugene seem to run or know something about running, so they truly respect the sport. They know enough not to offer the runners water, or to step onto the course to take a picture, or to impede us any other way. I always get a lot of calm, friendly support in Eugene.

The marathon had another attraction as well: it was the height of blackberry season in Oregon. I'd picked strawberries over the summer and blueberries in late August, so I wanted some blackberries to round out my jam larder.

I don't know exactly what made me run the OTC the way I did that day; perhaps it was the prospect of fruit bushes or the perfect weather. Whatever the inspiration, I ran my first sub-2:30 marathon in 2:26:11, a new American record. I felt the energy being passed to me from the fans as I got close to the finish line; even the Oregonians got excited when they realized I had a record. They are so much like Mainers— low-key and dignified—that I had to respond when I felt their collective emotion rise. It's not surprising that Oregon was settled mostly by New Englanders in the nineteenth century.

After the race I headed straight for the blackberry bushes and sat underneath one bush with a bucket. I picked alone for a while, but before too long I had some friends helping me. That evening I stashed the bucket, covered with tinfoil, under my airplane seat. Throughout the flight to Boston I noticed people sniffing the air, trying to find the source of the terrific smell.

There are unexpected surprises that come with marathon-ing. Now and again I see something, and the image is fixed in my brain. When I read about poverty in Mexico and illegal immigration, for example, I think back to a race in October 1982. This was the Crime Stoppers Run in El Paso, Texas. Once again, I had to leave Boston late because of B.U. du-ties. It didn't help that I slept that night in a room with a clock that bonged on the half hour and cuckooed on the hour. But I had enough in me to win the race.

What I remember best is the course. The race dipped south and traveled through Mexico for a couple of miles. As soon as we crossed the border we were running in an area of shocking poverty; it was difficult to accept the fact that the Rio Grande and a patrolled gate literally marked the border between life and death. Trite but true. We ran to hoots and catcalls, since the Mexicans were hardly accustomed to see-ing runners, much less female runners. As we pounded back into the States, dozens of Mexicans tried to join us. Some were in running clothes, but most were dressed normally, expressing a desperate faith in our numbers. The impulse was to shield them. We ran on, however, and the Immigra-tion people did their jobs. The experience was disturbing, but it was the sort of unpredictable lesson that I've learned to be grateful for.

I won the Rosemont Turkey Trot in Illinois on November 21 with an unofficial time of 31:44. Immediately after it I went to Bloomington, Indiana, to catch up with B.U.'s Marty Shea, who'd qualified for the NCAA national cross-country championships. Though she finished well back in the pack, it was great to see a member of the team reach a goal. Work-ing with them made me think about something besides my-self; self-absorption is a great danger to those who participate in solitary activities like running. B.U. didn't win a lot of meets, but it was improving.

My strategy for 1983 was to keep running races of differing lengths. The International Olympic Committee had announced the inclusion of the marathon for women at the next year's Los Angeles Games, and that was my primary aim, but I hoped to qualify for the 3,000 too. With this in mind, I won the 3,000m at a TAC meet in Boston in January and the mile at a Boston Track Club meet a month later, running my best time, 4:36.48. It was reassuring to know I could be competitive at a distance that should have been out of my range.

In the middle of February my Bowdoin coach, Frank Sabasteanski, died. I knew he had been ill with cancer, but he was one of those people for whom you somehow expect a miracle. I was training in Brookline when it happened. At one point in the run I suddenly felt hollow. I kept going, even though I had to battle for every step, thinking maybe the heavy traffic was getting me down. Scott called shortly after I finished my run and told me about Sabe; it sounds spooky, but I must have felt his passing during my run. I wouldn't believe that story unless it happened to me; I'm no spirit medium, but I was close to the coach and maybe he did visit me while I was on the road. He was one of the few people I knew who was still sizing me up after the 1979 Boston Marathon. As I sat through his funeral mass I remembered running past him on Pickard Field at Bowdoin. We used to go around the track, through the goalposts, and out onto the roads. As we left the field Sabe always had something to suggest that might improve my running. He was never completely satisfied with my style. I needed people like him to keep me honest; there was nobody to replace him when he was gone.

By March I was ready to run at the cross-country championships in Gateshead, England. I went out on the country roads with Kenny Moore, who was covering the meet for

Sports Illustrated. It was a long, difficult practice—I didn't want Kenny to think I couldn't keep up with him—but I felt good. Maybe I was unwise to run that hard the day before the race: I came in fourth. But I was the first American to finish and the U.S. team won the overall title. And that workout with Kenny convinced me that I was ready for the Boston Marathon.

Allison Roe was expected to win, but Jacqueline Gareau and Mary Shea were regarded as threats. I was given a chance; but despite my string of wins, I don't think people realized how strong I felt. Most people believed my heels would do me in on the hilly course. Winning a marathon in Oregon was one thing; winning in legendary Boston was another. Being lightly regarded made me work harder, and it also let me train in relative anonymity. There were few demands on my time for interviews and appearances. In any case, my involvement at B.U. kept me close to home.

Some good friends realized I was shooting for a sub-2:25 marathon. I talked to my former Liberty A.C. teammate Susan Hughes, who was working for Nike in Boston, to Scott, and to Bob Sevene. When they worried that I was keeping up too hectic a pace at B.U. and might get sick, I told them to relax. Everything in my body was peaking; I could have shaken off the plague.

On April 18 the "elite" runners met in the Hopkinton church basement and glanced sideways at one another. I think my competitors knew I'd spent the time since my Achilles surgery building toward a crescendo and that this might be it. I could win or lose the race spectacularly—with the training I was putting in, there was no safe middle ground. With that in mind, Allison Roe called me the day before the race to tell me that in London, Grete Waitz had just tied Allison's record of 2:25:29, which she had held since the

1981 New York Marathon. She suggested we join together in an attempt for a new world's best. I told her I wanted to run my own race and if we wound up running parts of the race together that was fine, but I wasn't about to alter my pre-race plans. Deep down I wanted a 2:25, but I wanted it for me, because I thought I was in shape for it, and not because I was panting after a record. I went into the race prepared to be mentally alone.

Sunday night I had a dream I've since identified as the type of premonition I'll have if I'm going to do well in a race. I'm lost, either in a department store or in a small village. In the department store version, I end up running up and down escalators and crashing through racks of clothing to escape. In the village, I have to jump through windows and over thresholds. The principle is the same—the cause of my panic is that I've missed the start of the race. I hear the gun go off and I run in circles. Finally I escape and join the pack. I have to run wildly to catch up with the leaders. (I am known for sleeping in and showing up at a race at the eleventh hour, but I only do that because my dreams wear me out, not because I want to drive the officials crazy.)

I woke up from the village dream drained emotionally, but by the time I reached Hopkinton I'd replaced the panic of the dream with a sort of detached grimness.

Kevin Ryan, a 1976 and 1980 New Zealand Olympic marathoner, was hired by a Boston radio station to cover the race from the course. He told me in the church he'd be out there running with us, but I think he was just making a courtesy call. He attached himself to his countrywoman, Allison Roe, plainly believing she would win. That gave me the last little jolt of determination I needed. After the gun sounded, I zoomed to a first-mile time of 4:47.

I know I'm enjoying a good race when I see the five-mile

marker go by and think, "Already?" If I notice the earlier markers, I'm in trouble. If I look back to see where my competitors are, that's just another way of saying "Come and get me." And if I check my watch frequently, it's because I'm wondering how much longer I have to suffer. Recently I've given up wearing a watch in competition—it distracts me. Many runners depend heavily upon their split times as indicators of how the race is going, but I try not to. I've known runners who allow a poor early split to destroy the whole race; they think a missed split will damage their time so much that it can't be made up. But a race can be salvaged by running a faster split later. I have to go with the flow so I don't get caught in traps of my own devising, which is why I don't plan elaborate race strategies.

In Boston the conditions were right for me. The temperature was in the fifties, the sky was cloudy, and the wind was from the west. Since I expected Allison to sit on my shoulder through the race and then try to pass me in the last miles, exploiting my lack of kick, I was determined to get enough ahead of her to undermine her strategy. Therefore, I didn't notice any mile markers for a long time, and by then I was running so smoothly they were irrelevant.

At 10k Kevin Ryan abandoned Allison and hustled to join me. My split at that point was 31:53 (one of the male runners I passed at three miles said, "Watch it, lady," because I was moving so fast). Since Kevin was in so-so shape—he'd expected the winning woman's pace to be 2:25–2:30—and since I was literally blistering my feet, his commentary became more and more spare as time went on. He had to conserve his breath to stay with me. All of which makes it patently ridiculous to say, as some did afterward, that Kevin had paced me. If anything, the pace car, which was right there with us, was setting the rhythm. Kevin was not acting as a coach, formally or informally. He, in fact, was a nuisance. He knew he was being a pain, but his job was to run along beside me and tell his listeners how he supposed I felt and what he thought my strategy was. He didn't ask me any questions and I didn't talk to him. I tried to forget he was there so he wouldn't sap my concentration.

In Wellesley, at about the sixteen-mile mark, I developed a side stitch. That threw my stride off and I slowed down. I don't know what would have happened if I'd been able to continue at the clip I was running up to that point: maybe I would have fallen apart on the hills, maybe I would have run a 2:20. The point is moot. The pain bothered me enough to change my pace, and I hit the hills with plenty of energy to spare. I later learned that Allison Roe dropped out at approximately the spot where I felt my side stitch. There must be a gremlin in Wellesley.

It wasn't too bad going up Heartbreak Hill and the others, but coming down was difficult. The bottoms of my feet were raw and sore. My heels bothered me as I ran into Cleveland Circle—I may have strained them by blasting through the beginning of the race, which was mostly downhill and, as such, tempted me to speed. My legs wobbled alarmingly on one downhill stretch and I thought maybe that was the end, but the finish line was close, now, and I couldn't give up. I recovered my composure, checked to see that the rest of my body could take the last five miles, and put myself on automatic pilot, aiming for the Prudential Center.

I stirred from my reverie only once. I heard my name called loudly and insistently from up ahead and flicked a glance in the direction of the noise. Most of the B.U. women's track team was perched on top of the subway station roof in Coolidge Corner, two miles from the finish line. They were screaming and jumping up and down on the precarious structure, and I dedicated the final miles to them.

By now it seemed clear that I had a world best, barring an

accident in the last mile. I could hear the race announcer yelling as I rounded the final corner and came down the last hill to the finish. He shouted himself hoarse, repeating my name over and over, whipping my "hometown" crowd into a frenzy. Male runners ahead parted to give me the center of the road. My broad smile, composed of equal parts of affection and relief, was genuine. I just love Boston and its marathon, and it felt so good to set a world record there. Records are supposed to be unattainable in those hills, but I had mine. It was 2:22:43. (When she saw a newspaper photo of my exhausted face after the marathon, Mom wrote me: "Joanie, if marathons make you look like this, please don't run any more.")

I was flying until the early hours of the following morning. In 1979 I had to be practically carried from the finish line, but this year I nearly skipped off the course. I was led to the receiving stand to get my medal; then, still sweaty, wrapped in a silver paper blanket, I attended the obligatory news conference with the second- and third-place finishers, Jacqueline Gareau (2:29:27) and Mary Shea (2:33:23). Scott reached through the sheeting the press people had set up for a backdrop and plucked me out of my chair for a mammoth hug and kiss ("Who was that masked man?" somebody joked). When he let me go I somehow answered the dozens of questions from all over the room. I couldn't account for taking nearly three minutes off the previous world best—all I could say was that I'd felt great and run the way I felt. I had a massage and a meal, and Scott and I danced into the next morning at the 57 Club. This time I was ready for the public attention, and I wasn't worried about my ability to handle it.

The effect of the win on the Boston University team was gratifying. We were close by now, and, as I've said, we were gaining inspiration from each other. I have never seen a more excited group of women. That spring, my actions did what I'd hoped my words would accomplish all along: they showed the team how to be tough and hungry. B.U. had a marvelous season, placing higher than ever before in the Eastern championship meet, and it was a pleasure to help coach the team. But at the end of the semester I decided to move back to Maine to pursue my dream of qualifying for the Olympics.

That summer I moved to Freeport, where I'd bought an old house the winter before. The remainder of 1983 produced mixed, but generally favorable, running results. I could have done myself some harm by running a 10k in Kalamazoo on April 30. It was too soon after Boston to be practical, and it was a rainy, miserable day. Luck was with me, though—I won that and many subsequent races. I knew I was tired, but I had plenty of adrenaline always at the ready.

The TAC Nationals were in mid-June, and in the 3,000m trials I was third behind Mary Decker and Allison Wiley, but I beat Francie Larrieu for the first time. Two days later, in the finals, I ran a personal best 8:53.49, but finished sixth; nonetheless, I consider this one of my best efforts ever.

In July I set a new course record at the Crain's Challenge 12k in Ithaca, Illinois, and took first place in the Bix 7 road race in Iowa. August found me in Falmouth once again, winning with a new record of 36:21. Four days later I won the 3,000m at the Pan Am Games in Caracas, but my time was a disappointing 9:14. I took a sluggish lead at the 400-meter mark and ran alone from then on, seeing no reason to push myself. The conditions in Caracas were far from desirable; the athletes' village was never completed.

I came in first in the Philadelphia Distance Run in September, taking the 13.1-mile course in 1:09:16 and setting a new American record. At the ProComfort 10k in Brookline I found myself in a gritty race with Jan Merrill. She stayed right behind me for four miles and I don't know how my legs delivered the power I needed, but I won in 32:22.

I was victorious in two 10k's in October and November. By December I was exhausted enough to take it easy. I slid into a small letdown. My heels were sore, my training loops were stale, I couldn't get excited about much of anything. The questions I was trying to ignore kept springing at me when I let my guard down: What if you don't make the team? What if your Achilles can't take it?

Just when I needed to shift my focus and haul myself out of the blue pits, there was Scott. He'd been around all the time, of course, but on December 18 he proposed. He asked a half-crazed athlete to be his wife. I said yes before he could change his mind.

As 1983 ended, the thought that was uppermost in my mind was that I had the opportunity to make some dreams come true in 1984. By October of that year, I would be Mrs. Scott Samuelson and (perhaps) an Olympian. It seemed too good to be true. It almost was.

NINE

When I moved to Freeport I had to dump several big cardboard boxes full of my belongings in the various rooms on the first floor because I couldn't unpack them. Most of the house was to be gutted and rebuilt before I could think about where to put things. Because there was no insulation upstairs, I was confined to living on the first floor, which had a bedroom, living room, kitchen, and bathroom. In summer the upstairs rooms were like flyblown ovens; in the winter, despite the heavy plastic I bought to cover every window, I could have used the same rooms as annexes to my refrigerator. I never went upstairs unless I was giving a tour.

Nike wanted to film a commercial in the quaint, rustic setting. When Rob Strasser and Pam Magee from Nike arrived, they said, "We can't film anything here. This place doesn't even have front steps." They kept asking if I was really living there. The commercial was eventually made in Westchester County, New York: quaint, but not too rustic.

Other crews did brave the conditions to work with me in Freeport. In January ABC filmed a profile piece on me to have on hand for their Olympic coverage in case I made the

Olympics. The network people were more comfortable working at my brother Andy's house in Boothbay, but they got some good shots of Scott and me ripping apart the outside of the house while my black labrador puppy, Creosote, played in the snow. They were followed by other network and independent crews, none of whom could credit my lifestyle. They were from the Big City, I told myself, and didn't understand that most Mainers lived in conditions worse than mine.

Creosote and I made do with what we had. I bought him in November, so he and I went through the first winter together feeling as hardy as Pilgrims. Cre had it easier than some of my houseguests: there was a week or so in January when I was without plumbing while the system was being worked on; at the time, I was trying to housebreak Creosote on newspapers in the living room, but more often than not he hit the green rug. At least he didn't have to go outside, as did we humans. I have a mental picture of him pressing his nose against the window and snickering as he watched the humans head off into the frigid woods when there was a perfectly good rug available.

I had some trouble getting the contractor to work himself into my schedule. If I had to be away for a week, that was certain to be the time his men couldn't work in Freeport. The house was in an uproar for almost a year. I never knew what was going to happen next. The experience with the house helped me adjust to a series of unpredictable problems. I even learned to catch a nap while the walls were being torn down around me.

I had every reason to think that the sentiments my parents inscribed in the *New Yorker Diary* they gave me for Christmas would be affirmed in 1984. My mother wrote: "May this year be as good to you as the year before. Take care of yourself and enjoy each day. Love, Dad and Mother." In spite of the hubbub at home, I was living as quietly as I could and putting in over a hundred miles of training every week. I knew I was approaching the best shape of my life.

In February I ran the 3,000m at the Olympic Invitational track meet at the Meadowlands in New Jersey. Suzanne Girard won; I was second by a very close margin, an adequate performance. My training was not yet in high gear and I didn't feel as fast as I had in 1983, when I lost the same race to Patti-Sue Plummer by an even closer margin.

I was careful to tell my friends (and myself) that I was putting in a lot of solitary training miles, aiming for the marathon trials. I wanted only to make the Olympic team—anything more would be gravy. My deepest wishes stayed buried; it wouldn't do to get all worked up about an Olympic race I might never run. Friends playfully slugged me on the shoulder and as much as said, "But we all know you'll be in L.A." The fact was, I didn't know. I wanted to get to Olympia, Washington, for the trials. L.A. could take care of itself.

On March 17 I drove to Cape Elizabeth so I could run the twenty-mile loop that was the best indicator of my fitness. I'd been running that loop since the first time I tried the distance; it was completely familiar. When I ran it well, I knew I was in excellent condition. This day I expected to do better than ever: my training was paying off by then and I felt glorious.

At Meetinghouse Hill in South Portland, about seventeen miles into the run, I had a sensation in my knee. It was as if a spring were unraveling in the joint. The knee became sore immediately and I veered off my normal course and altered my stride. I hobbled along for two miles, but I finally had to start walking a quarter mile from home. The farther I went, the tighter the knee got—something seemed to be obstructing its movement.

When I reached my parents' house I was a wreck. By some act of Providence Mom wasn't there to see my condition; every time I suffer an injury she feels the pain. I don't think she could have stood seeing me panic. This was the most frightening moment of my life, and the first time I ever panicked as an athlete. I knew the problem wasn't muscular: it happened too quickly. One moment I was fine, the next I was limping. Muscle injuries give you the luxury of adequate warning, unless the muscle is turned or pulled abruptly. Nothing in my fluid running that day would have led to a muscle strain. This was something alarmingly, paralyzingly different. I wasn't thinking clearly, but I remember the fear vividly. I was like an artist who crafts a masterpiece over the course of ten years and then sees it consumed in a sudden fire. She wonders what the ashes will reveal and is afraid she won't be able to replace the work of art.

Bob Sevene was visiting his mother in Massachusetts and planned to be in Freeport that afternoon. (He was still living and coaching in Eugene and would stay at Athletics West until the fall of 1986.) I couldn't wait that long. I called him from the heap I was in and told him what had happened. He kept his voice steady and suggested I take it easy. Sev was once quoted as saying, "My problem has always been holding runners back, getting them to cut down on mileage or take a day off. All runners seem to push themselves too hard."

Sev calmed me down and convinced me to call Dr. Leach. It was Friday afternoon, though, so I decided to stay off the knee for a day and see how it felt on Sunday. If it didn't improve, I'd call Dr. Leach on Monday.

I walked around all day Saturday and the knee didn't

bother me, so on Sunday I tried an eleven-mile run. The knee tightened up and became sore in the last mile, but I was optimistic enough to think it was getting better. On Monday morning I ran a very familiar six-mile loop in Freeport and felt okay. But that afternoon I set out on the same loop and hadn't gone a half mile before the pain stopped me. I arranged to see Dr. Leach the next day.

I wanted to say to him, "I think there's something floating around in there, obstructing the joint," but I'm not an orthopedic surgeon and it wasn't my place to tell him what to look for. He injected the knee with cortisone and told me to back off for a few days. He said, "I'm going to be in charge of the [Olympic] team physicians and I want to see you with a medal around your neck." That made two of us.

I felt fine for the next couple of weeks. I ran fifteen to twenty miles daily and did track and Nautilus workouts besides. Naturally, I thought the problem was solved. The knee was still a bit tender, but I could run with it, and that was the only thing that mattered.

Everything came tumbling down on April 10. I took a long run in the morning and, always hopeful, recorded in my diary, "No knee pain." At seven that evening I had a track workout at Harvard, where I ran three sub–five-minute miles and felt terrific. I stopped to talk to John Babington before doing my cool-down laps, and when I began running again, there was the lock. It got tighter with each lap. The next morning I went out for a ten-mile run with a friend. I got to the subway station on Commonwealth Avenue near Boston College and had to stop; I wanted to gut it out, but something in the knee just wasn't right. I apologized to my friend and told him to go ahead because I'd have to walk from there. Later I called Dr. Leach and said I hated to be a pain in the neck, but I thought he'd better take another look at the pain in my knee. He gave me an appointment for the next day.

Always wanting to test myself, I ran twelve miles Thursday morning before seeing Dr. Leach. My diary entry says it all: "Last 3 + miles were completely miserable. Would have walked if I had had the time but was probably going through the motions of running slower than I would have walked. A real effort to lift my right leg over a twig." And that was no exaggeration—I remember stopping at every curb to step off with my left foot and drag the right down behind it.

Dr. Leach gave me another shot of cortisone. We both knew time was running out: the trials were slated for May 12 and it was now April 12. He told me to take three or four days off. As always, I treated his words as gospel; I could only hope that the rest and medication would solve the problem.

I swam and lifted weights to stay in shape; the stationary bicycle bothered the knee. I knew I wasn't getting the kind of cardiovascular workout I needed to keep my edge, but anything was better than sitting around brooding. Lots of times I thought, "Why bother to go on? This isn't going to work"; then I'd go exercise to lift the depression. I couldn't give in to the fear that was just waiting for a weak moment to break through and take over.

On April 14 I flew to Tucson for meetings with the Dole sales force. I had just signed on as a spokesperson and fitness consultant for Dole pineapple juice. In Arizona I really began to fret; the knee was tightening up even while I walked, especially if I walked downhill. I spoke to the group on Monday and tried to run with them on Tuesday, but my mind was focused on my problem. I don't know how I got through those two days. After running on Tuesday I wrote, "Right knee not right. Tight, catching feeling seemed to subside a little into the run but certainly not to the extent that I could have opened stride enough to run smoothly. Flew to Eugene."

There are no further entries in my running log until the day of the Olympic trials. I couldn't bear to write about my problems. I tried to adjust to things as they arose, but all along something in my brain was muttering, "If we don't think about this, it might go away." Writing it would have put the lie to that hope.

Escaping to Oregon seemed like a good idea—maybe a few massage sessions and some physical therapy would work things out. Bob Sevene was at the airport to meet me, and we drove straight to Dr. Stan James's office, hoping he would be the miracle man I needed. Again, I wanted to come right out and say, "Listen, I know this is mechanical," but, again, how do you tell a highly respected orthopedic surgeon what to do? After he examined the knee he told me any number of things could be wrong and he didn't want to do anything rash, like operate, until I rested it for five more days.

Bob took me to the Athletics West office building and I had to fight back the tears all the way. When we got there I went to the ladies' room and broke down. Mary Angelico, with whom I would stay in Oregon, found me there and held me. I kept telling her I knew something was wrong and this wasn't the time for resting, not with the trials so close. "This is ridiculous," I sobbed. "I shouldn't be this upset. This is only running. I could be dying of cancer."

That was Wednesday. On Saturday I was so antsy I had to test things. Every day I didn't run robbed me of fitness, even though I was exercising however I could. I ran two or three miles on the Amazon Trails in Eugene with Bob Sevene before the knee shut down. I thought my heart would break.

On Easter Sunday I went to mass in the morning and asked God why He had sent this injury to me at this time. Why me? Why now? After praying those questions I looked across the church and saw Alberto Salazar. At first I was jealous of his health; Alberto had been prone to injuries in the past, but he was ready for the trials. Then, when my envy passed, I reconfirmed what I'd always believed: that God has a reason for everything He does. The whole situation was in His hands, not mine. I prayed, then, that if I couldn't run in the trials and Olympics, God would grant Alberto the two best races of his life.

The next day Stan James called Dr. Leach and consulted with him. I don't think he was comfortable with the ethical ramifications of taking over my case, but I was desperate and Leach was in Boston. After my history was carefully described to him, Stan decided to get an arthroscope into my knee and see what was wrong. That made me happier than I'd been in two months. Finally, there would be action—no more passive therapy. I think we were all worried that Stan might not find anything in there, which would mean I'd have the original problem plus a surgical wound, but I was sure the problem could be solved with surgery.

I think everyone figured there was no way I'd be able to run the marathon on May 12 but supposed I might be in shape for the 3,000 at the track trials in Los Angeles in June. I didn't have a great chance of making the team at that distance—I wasn't world class in the 3,000—but there was always hope.

That afternoon I ran with a brace made of wetsuit material on my knee, but the joint locked anyway. I called Andy that night and said I was going ahead with surgery; he thought I should try more rest, and his doubts gave me a few seconds of pause, but then I said, "I have to be the one to decide what the risks are and whether they are worth taking."

The next day I was set up for surgery in a pre-op room and told I would wake up there or in Recovery. I was supposed to leave the hospital that day. But I regained consciousness in a regular hospital room. I was scared, thinking something major had been found in my knee and further surgery would be necessary. I lifted my head to take a look at my leg—it was wrapped in elastic bandages. That was a relief. In my doped-up condition, I'd almost believed they had lopped the leg off. There was no feeling in it, but as long as it was there I figured I could use it: I called Mary Angelico and asked her to pick me up on her way home from work so I could go running. She said, "Uh-huh, yeah, sure, Joanie," and hung up.

When my head was clear Stan James told me I was being held in the hospital overnight to keep the swelling to a minimum (he knew too well what I might do to his handiwork if he let me out of his sight). The procedure had turned up a fibrous mass, called a plica, which had become inflamed and interfered with the joint. Stan had to look carefully, scoping up and down each tendon, before he found it; the correction was prompt and uncomplicated.

He told me not to run until he saw me a week later, on the thirtieth. I could swim at the Eugene YMCA and pedal a stationary bicycle slowly, but that was the only exercise I was allowed.

I avoided reporters; I was afraid they might talk me out of trying to run. I knew my chances were slim, but as long as the possibility existed I needed all of my confidence to make the effort.

Which is where my fellow athletes came in. Many runner friends called me over the next few days, and there was a mountain of mail. Other athletes wrote to say they hoped an exception would be made for me if I couldn't run in the trials; one woman said: "If I could run as fast as you and qualify, I'd give you my berth."

In Beaverton on the twenty-ninth, the day before I had my appointment with Dr. James, I couldn't stand the suspense anymore; I ran a little and everything was fine. I worked out in the Nike weight room that afternoon, then drove to Eugene. The next day Dr. James gave me a green light to run if I promised to start slowly, which I did. The next day I roamed Eugene at a leisurely pace.

On May 2, however, I woke up saying, "I'm back to normal. I'm going to start running." The knee was fixed. I had to get on with it if I wanted to be on the starting line in Olympia on May 12. My daily schedule from then on was grueling. Mary would wake me at six a.m. and take me to the weight room, then she would do aerobics while I rode a bike or sat in the whirlpool. After that she dropped me off at the Y for a swim and one of my Athletics West teammates, Dan Dillon or Larry Mangan, picked me up from there and took me to a physical therapy session. I spent several hours a day in therapy and also ran as much as I could. Most days I didn't get back to the apartment until eleven at night. I was so eager to make up for lost time that I forgot my promise to Stan James and pushed myself harder than I had since the knee problem first cropped up. But I was still nervous about the knee and favored my right leg. The result was a pulled hamstring in the left leg. Instantly, the knee was downgraded from a major problem to something that wasn't even relevant anymore: if anything was going to keep me out of the trials now, it would be the hamstring.

My mood stayed upbeat; I tried to cope with the new emergency. I added hamstring treatment to my knee rehab therapy. Part of the therapy I could do at home with Tens, a form of electrical stimulation. Larry Standifer, a physical therapist, gave me a little black box with electrodes sticking out of it and told me how to attach them to the knee and hamstring. I was supposed to use the device when I had some free time, so I would clamp it on while Mary and I were eating dinner late at night. Once in a while I turned the juice up too high and my leg would start flopping all over the place as I yelled and fumbled for the knobs. For a person who didn't like quirky remedies, I was putting myself through a lot to regain my fitness.

Even with ice therapy as part of my routine, the leg was still sore. On May 4 I ran with Sev and Doug Brown, who at the time was Athletics West's team administrator, and though they maintained an easy pace, I could only stay with them for two miles. The next day I attended a track meet at Hayward Field at the University of Oregon. It was frustrating to watch people run smoothly when I couldn't think of competing. I was so desperate for a solution by then that Dick Brown, Mary Decker's coach at that time, introduced me to Jack Scott, who was attending the meet to try out his Myopulse and Electron Acuscope. These were new treatments Mary had used with some success for pulls and tendonitis. Once again my attitude was "What have I got to lose?" I had a four-hour treatment that night and went for five days more of six to ten hours of treatment per day. In order to accommodate these long treatment sessions I had to cut out all activity except for early-morning swims.

I still didn't feel right, but I slowly started to run. On May 9, three days before the trials, I gave myself a short speech: "This is it. You have to go out and run at least fifteen miles. If you can't, there's no way you're going to run in the trials." I ran two repeat loops that day for a total of sixteen miles. I was so unsure of my footing that I had to concentrate to put one foot in front of the other—it was like working a marionette. My stride was way off; there was nothing fluid in my motion. Running was a huge effort, and I knew if I overdid it I could rip the hamstring. The one consolation—besides making my goal—was my strong cardiovascular condition.

I'd been on the phone daily to Scott since the whole business began, of course, but that night he came to Eugene and I thought, "Now I'll be okay." Having him there to hold on to would make things turn out fine. The next morning we ran together and I felt wonderful.

Peter and Andy and Andy's wife, Stevie, came to watch me run in Olympia. Earlier in the week, before Scott had arrived, I had told them not to come because things didn't look promising. They arrived anyway, under the guise of a vacation in the Pacific Northwest.

Even as I was jogging to the starting line, I honestly didn't know whether I could manage the race. I don't think the other competitors gave me a chance of finishing. But when I spotted Scott and my brothers and sister-in-law climbing into the van that would take them to the first checkpoint, I vowed to pull it off somehow.

I began to run as conservatively as possible, because I felt immediate pain and weakness in the hamstring. I tried to ignore it by taking in the scenery on the quiet course as it wound through the state capital. It was easy to imagine that this was Maine—there was plenty of water to look at, crisp spring breezes blew, and I could pretend I was on a loop in Freeport. Only the spectators and my worries about the knee and the hamstring broke the pleasant reverie, because I wasn't aiming to win the race. Third place would be fine; the first three finishers would qualify.

For the first three or four miles I ran with the leaders and let them set the pace. Then Betty Jo Springs, who I thought would win, and I broke away from the pack. I passed her, she passed me, and we continued on that way until mile fourteen, never more than a couple of steps apart. At this point I took the lead for good. I knew I had to get well in front and hope my momentum would carry me to the finish line, since I could tell my legs wouldn't have anything left for a surge at the end. I still expected Betty Jo or maybe Julie Brown to pass me, but they never appeared.

In the last six miles I ran slower and slower, showing the disjointedness of my training. There were lots of turns in the course and I had to be especially careful about the way I planted my feet on them to avoid excess torque on the knee and hamstring. Miraculously, my legs held up and I finished first in 2:31:04. Julie Brown was second at 2:31:41, and Julie Isphording third.

When I crossed the finish line I broke into sobs in Sev's arms. The television people were right there, so I pulled myself together and told them what was in my heart: that without the support of family and friends, I wouldn't have made the race. They had crashed through my self-imposed isolation in the days preceding the race to tell me they were there with me. Theirs were the voices that spoke simple facts—that I would be valuable to them with or without Olympic dreams; that Maine was there waiting for me, as always; and that they would be taking every step with me at Olympia. Because I was buoyed by these people, I ran what I still consider to be the race of my life that day. They helped me find a miracle.

I've often been asked whether I think an exception should have been made for me if I hadn't been able to qualify in the trials. It is true that, given the time between the arthroscopic surgery and the Olympic Marathon, I would have had a chance to get healthy at a reasonable pace. I knew I'd be fine in another month. Fred Lebow, the director of the New York Marathon, told the press he thought both Alberto Salazar and I should get automatic marathon berths because we had world bests; Jacqueline Hansen, Doris Heritage Brown (the coach of the female Olympic qualifiers in Washington), and others who were highly respected in the sport put in their pleas, but the U.S. Olympic Committee held fast. Thank goodness. Even at my lowest ebb, I knew I should not ask for special treatment. Other athletes had experienced similar problems in previous years and the rules should not be changed. The trials are a tough school, but to choose Olympic teams on the basis of past records is to invite favoritism and politics.

Over the next several weeks in Maine my training was sluggish; the summer was unusually hot. But with the Olympic Marathon in early August it was easy to persuade myself to work hard. I traveled as infrequently as possible, preferring to put in my hundred-mile weeks on thoroughly familiar loops.

I did go to New York to appear with Grete Waitz on "Good Morning America." She was there for the L'eggs Mini, and even though I wasn't in the race, GMA thought it would be interesting to interview us together. Much was being made of the fact that the Olympics would be our first meeting as marathoners. We had breakfast after the show and talked about our training and the race in Los Angeles. By then Grete was very comfortable in the United States and her English was perfect, so she was more relaxed than I'd ever seen her. But we were both excited at the prospect of competing.

On June 17 I ran in the Olympic Trials Exhibition 10,000-meter race, which was held in the L.A. Coliseum. I won the event in 32:07, which convinced me that I was fully recovered. The race itself was symbolic, because it had not yet been approved as an Olympic event, but it will be included at Seoul in 1988. Symbolic or not, I won by a considerable margin and was eager to come back to Los Angeles the following month.

When I returned there on July 23 for the Olympics I was told that my quarters were at the University of Southern California Olympic Village. I should have stayed in the Village and absorbed the entire ambience of the Games, but the athletes were allowed to make alternate arrangements as long as the officials knew our whereabouts. Since my dorm was next to the swimming pool, where the first events would take place, I was afraid the excitement would get my adrenaline flowing too early. So Jacqueline Hansen found a place for me with Sherrill Kushner and Ed Klein in Santa Monica. They had a small guesthouse, and I could come and go without disturbing them.

Everything was perfect until I went out to run—it seemed as if all the Olympic athletes were training in Santa Monica. The cyclists zoomed along San Vicente Boulevard overtaking the runners, who then turned to training on the gorgeous beaches. It was an ideal setting, but my face and reputation had preceded me and every time I went out for a run somebody challenged me to race. I felt like Gregory Peck in *The Gunfighter*. I should have ignored the challenges, but my competitiveness rose to every occasion. Before long I was tired and knew I had to get away. I decided to stay until the opening ceremonies, then fly back to Oregon for some peace.

On the day of the opening ceremonies, I got to USC in time to throw my stuff in my room, change, and head out to the track for a few strides. My way was blocked, however, by several security people. I couldn't get to the track because President Reagan's helicopter was scheduled to land in the infield in an hour or so; he was going to address the assembled athletes before we went on to the Coliseum. I got lost, finding that I couldn't take familiar paths because they were too close to the President's chosen route, and thereby missed the team picture. But I was back in time to hear Mr. Reagan speak. When he finished we were loaded onto buses and driven to the Coliseum.

What I said to the policeman in Brookline was equally true of this trip across Los Angeles: I could have run faster than we were driving. The city was filled with people trying to reach the Olympic stadium. We finally made it and were marched into a building near the Coliseum to watch the opening ceremonies on a huge TV screen. There would be a long wait in the program before the parade of nations was to begin.

As soon as they turned on the screen it malfunctioned and nobody could repair it. The athletes missed the Gershwin number and everything else that came before our entrance. We became bored and restless. Already worked up with emotion, the last thing we needed was a bad omen. But everyone made the best of it; the noise in the hall grew deafening as we circulated, trading team pins with athletes from different countries. It was a scene.

As the hall cleared for the parade the Americans got together in small groups and vented our complaints about the ugly uniforms we were wearing. Various team managers, coaches, and officials from the USOC told us to wait until we saw all the uniforms together. And when we lined up, forming a field of red, white, and blue, I understood what they meant. It really was magnificent.

To get to the Coliseum we had to walk through the same tunnel the marathoners would enter to run their final lap on the track. I thought how terrific it would be if I came through here into a full stadium in first place. I didn't dwell on the possibility, though, not because I wasn't ready to run, but because the events of the evening made everything else fade. Marathon day might have been a year away. Like everything else, it was on hold during producer David Wolper's show.

We marched in and took our places on the infield. I had the shakes as I realized where I was; it is a moment I find difficult to describe. Gina Hemphill, Jesse Owens's granddaughter, bore the Olympic flame onto the track and hundreds of prohibited cameras were whipped out of our pockets as we surged toward her. The security people hissed at us to get back as poor Gina broke her stride time and again to outmaneuver the crowd. Finally she passed the torch to Rafer Johnson, who ran up the long staircase at the head of the stadium and touched off the flame that would burn throughout the Games. To call these minutes electric would be to understate the case; my whole body was tingling with awe and pride. Balloons and doves were released into the air. The crowd in the stands stomped and cheered. We held hands and sang "Reach Out and Touch"—Dr. Leach found me during the song and took my hand. I wish I had told him what I was thinking: "If it hadn't been for you and Dr. James, I wouldn't be here." But I was on the brink of tears; one word and the flood would start. I sang, hoping he'd hear the thanks in my voice.

When the ceremonies were over some of us raced out of the Coliseum, too pumped up to ride the slow buses back to USC. We jogged on air all the way to our rooms. I decided to sleep in the Village that night, and the next day I went to Eugene.

I was feeling so good and so fast that it was all I could do

to hold myself back in my training. When I'm in that condition I want to run until I drop. Bob Sevene was there to
remind me that the Olympic race would suffer if I pushed
myself too hard. It was difficult to find alternatives to running. Mary Angelico and I tried playing Scrabble, but I
couldn't keep my mind on it and drove her crazy by jumping
up and down to get the phone or do my laundry in the
middle of a game.

The biggest drawback in preparing for the Olympics was
that it had kept me out of the berry fields in Maine, so I
picked lots of raspberries in Oregon to make jam for Christmas gifts. One morning Mary left the house just as I started
boiling jam, and when she got home the whole kitchen was
covered with it and I was out for a run. One of her roommates answered the telephone and his ear stuck to the re-
ceiver. As he wiped the jam off his head he turned to Mary
and said, "*When* is she going to L.A.?"

On August 3 Sev and Rich Phaigh (the Athletics West
masseur) and Mary and I headed for the airport for the flight
to Los Angeles. I spotted some wooden toys in the airport
gift shop and Mary and I stopped to examine them while the
men boarded the plane. I found the perfect ornament for the
top of our wedding cake: a wooden boat with two people
sitting in it. Scott had built a boat for me as a birthday gift;
if we painted the toy boat green it would be an ideal minia-
ture. I took it to the counter, and as I was paying Mary
tugged on my sleeve and said, "Hey, do you know our plane
is leaving?" We just made it.

Then my carefully arrangéd facade began to collapse. I
was relaxed until the plane took off. When the captain told us
over the intercom about the weather in L.A. my stomach
began to hurt. An upset stomach is my perennial marathon
companion (I have that in common with Grete Waitz); this

one was bad enough to erase everything else from my mind. When the plane landed I had one goal—to find a bathroom. So much for Oregon and my composure.

I half sprinted to the restroom, head down, holding my stomach. All of a sudden I was stopped by a punk with purple and green hair; he grabbed my arm and held me. There were three others dressed in L.A.-punker garb with weird hairdos and metal things hanging off their ears. I was furious. I reared back to yell at them and the tall one who'd grabbed me said, "Oh, Joan," and I finally recognized Scott. The other "punks" were my brother John, his wife, Holly, and Martha Agan, who would soon be my matron of honor. (Martha was there because she'd written "When you get to the Olympics, I'll be your coach. Ha ha" in my high school yearbook. She added the "Ha ha" because when we were youngsters she always beat me in races up the hill to her house.) I laughed, but I also made Scott release me so I could run to the bathroom. The idea of the costumes was to break the tension, and it worked. My stomach problems didn't go away, but my song changed from the monotonous "I just can't deal" to "Let's get this show on the road."

I joined my family and relatives for a relaxing dinner before heading back to Sherrill and Ed's house to stay until the marathon. August 4 passed slowly; it was one of the few days in my life in which there were too many hours. That night I used the bathroom every half hour or so; I couldn't sleep. I lay in bed and listened to the theme from *Chariots of Fire* over and over again on a Walkman. I slept for about an hour and dreamed I was trapped in a department store.

Sunday, August 5, fifty of us gathered at Santa Monica College to start the race. The stands weren't filled, as I'd imagined they would be, and the day was gray, without distinct features. At first it all seemed like an anticlimax. My stomach was still bothering me, so I waited for the other athletes to vacate the stadium bathroom and cleared my system. When I emerged from the bathroom, officials were lining up the athletes for the march onto the track. The competitors were in alphabetical order according to the countries they represented. The U.S. marched last, as the host country. The athletes of each nation were lined up according to height. I took my position at—needless to say— the tail end of the group. It was at this time that I thought of something my mother had been saying for as long as I could remember: "First shall come last and last shall come first." There was a little music and some flag-waving; then we all milled around for a while. I couldn't focus; I heard popping sounds in my head, as if my brain were breaking free of its moorings before floating away. I worried that I'd have to make another pit stop before the race began. Jitters galore. There was some medication in a plastic bag attached to the inside of my shorts for me to take in the event of stomach problems, but once the gun went off I was darned if I was going to reach into my shorts on ABC television.

At last, we lined up and were sent on our way. I was wearing a white cap to keep the sun off my head, but it wasn't shining strongly yet. We were grateful to be running in the morning, before the city heated up and the smog reached choking levels. I actually wasn't bothered by the heat at all.

My memories are fragmentary. For the first three miles I ran with the pack, but then I decided to break away because I felt hemmed in. I couldn't stride properly surrounded by all the other runners. If I had to be the pacesetter in order to run my own race, that was fine. Right after I broke free the first water station came up, and I was darned if I was going to get into a crowd again just for a drink, so I skipped it.

Most of the others took water and I pulled farther away. I had prepared properly as far as drinking water in the days leading up to the marathon—as evidenced by my frequent bathroom trips the night before. Once we got past that station the lead was mine for good.

I couldn't believe the other runners weren't coming after me. I glanced over my shoulder a few times in the next two miles, expecting to see Grete Waitz or Ingrid Kristiansen or Rosa Mota within range, but no one appeared. It was like a dream: here I was, running comfortably and in control of the Olympic Marathon with no visible opposition. The gap widened as each mile ticked off.

Ingrid was quoted in *Sports Illustrated* as saying that she was waiting for Grete Waitz to make *her* move. "If I'd followed Joanie, maybe three or four other girls would have come too. It might have been a different race. But I waited for Grete."

I dreaded the stretch on the freeway. In Maine there is nothing that even approximates the highway system around Los Angeles. All my life I'd heard about the L.A. freeway in comedy monologues and from friends who lived in California. It was a great surprise to discover that the freeway stretch was the only part of the course that reminded me of Maine. There were no spectators allowed, so except for the pace car, I was alone. If I'd closed my eyes I could have pretended I was in Freeport. Next to the finish line, the freeway was my favorite part of the race.

Normally I am concentrating so intensely on my running that I register the details of a course only in retrospect, if at all. But when I looked over at the sidewalk in Marina del Rey and saw a black and white Bowdoin banner I had to grin. There's usually one Bowdoin banner somewhere in the crowd when I run a marathon and it always gives me a lift.

Not that I needed much inspiration. I've seen the video-tapes and I know the ABC commentators thought I had taken the lead rashly, too early. I admit I had one or two brief flashes of doubt and imagined the pack thundering by me in the last few miles. But when sixteen miles passed, then twenty, and I still felt completely in control, I knew I wasn't going to be caught. Unlike in the late stages of the trials, I was sure I could pick up my pace if need be.

The sun was beginning to show its face during the last miles and the temperature was rising, but nothing seemed to bother me. Runners often talk about their best races being their easiest races. The Olympic Marathon was that way for me.

Just before entering the ramp leading down into the Coliseum tunnel I took a quick look at a bigger-than-life mural of me finishing the 1983 Boston Marathon. Nike had commissioned an artist to paint the mural on a windowless side of a tall brick building. The building stood by itself outside the Coliseum, and here I was about to enter the stadium by myself. I had seen the wall painting the previous fall; I was a bit uncomfortable with it, but I think it played a positive role in my preparation for the Olympics.

Shortly after I looked away from the mural the tunnel was in sight. When I got close I could hear the crowd rumbling inside—they had been watching the race on a pair of giant screens and knew who and where I was. As I ran into the tunnel the noise was muffled and I heard my own footfalls. I thought, "Once you leave this tunnel your life will be changed forever." I fastened my eyes on my shoes and kept running.

My mother later said that I looked like a little gray mouse skittering out of a hole. The crowd bellowed as soon as I emerged into the sunlight to run the final lap. My legs were wobbly with emotion; I put my head down even further and said aloud, "You're not finished yet. Get around the track and nail this thing down." With about two hundred meters to go, I took off my cap and waved to the crowd. I was so charged up that when I broke the tape I could have turned around and run another twenty-six miles, though maybe not in a time of 2:24:52, a minute and a half ahead of Grete Waitz. Somebody from Nike handed me a big American flag that Bob Sevene's teenaged son Trent had brought to the Olympics and I took my victory lap trying to get it to unfurl in the strong breeze. My father vaulted out of the stands to join me on the track. I didn't see him, and the second he hit the ground a swarm of security people were there to stuff him back into his seat. The security force couldn't worry about who he was; it was their job to keep the athletes safe. Later he said he was glad he hadn't made it to the track.

When I finished jogging I was grabbed by ABC for a quick interview, and then I searched the stands for my parents. There was no hope of finding Scott—he was sitting with my brother John and Holly and Martha and Sev in the nosebleed section—but Mom and Dad had places down front, if I could just figure out where. I had a rough idea, but it was difficult to find them because everyone I looked at was smiling and waving. The first person to embrace me was Dr. Leach, who was close to the finish line. Several months earlier he had said he wanted to see me at the tape, and there we were.

After a few moments I located my parents and got the big hugs I wanted. From there I went to the medical compound to have my urine tested for drugs, and then Grete Waitz (second) and Rosa Mota (third) and I met the press. They all wanted to know how we felt about the collapse of Gabriela Andersen-Schiess, but none of us had seen her or heard what happened.

I met my parents at the USC sorority house Nike had rented, and I put my white hat on a table in the front room, but later it was gone. Somebody may have thrown it away, thinking it was a discard. Because Olympic tradition doesn't permit medals to be awarded until the afternoon, I had time for a massage and fun with family and friends before returning to the Coliseum for the presentation.

When the U.S. flag was raised over my head and the national anthem was played, I was beyond feeling. I had to take several long breaths to make it through the ceremony.

A true philatelist, I went straight to the Coliseum post office to get some envelopes postmarked for that day. I was sitting at a table making out the envelopes, concentrating on what I was doing, when I noticed a group of people, two and three deep, that had gathered around me. I signed autographs for a solid hour until I was rescued by friends.

The attention wears thin quickly, however, especially after such a highly charged race. On the night of the race the people from Dole threw a party for my family and friends that lasted until midnight. Then Scott, Martha, John, Holly, and I had a slumber party in John and Holly's hotel room during which no one slumbered. At 3:45 a.m. a limousine drove me to ABC's Los Angeles studios to appear on "Good Morning America." CBS picked me up after that so I could be on their news program, and then I was taken to NBC. A press conference followed in downtown L.A. When I emerged from that I could hardly breathe—the air quality was lousy. I attended yet another press conference before I was finally set free. I went to the Nike house and watched the Games on TV for the rest of the afternoon. The next day I shook off the fatigue with a nine-mile run in Santa Monica. The other runners on San Vicente Boulevard left me alone.

Some of my teammates told me that their hometowns were

planning welcoming parades and ceremonies. Since I wanted to return to life in Maine with as little fuss as possible, I decided to fly back unannounced on the eighth, three days after the marathon. I spent the night with Martha Agan and her husband, Jay. I couldn't stand any more bright lights.

My parents returned the same evening to a transformed house: on the front door there was a huge replica of a gold medal, and on the lawn was a sign reading "It all started here."

I went running on the outermost fringes of Cape Elizabeth the next day. I knew I'd cause a stir in the center of town, so I planned my route to take in farmlands and a couple of cemeteries. A police car passed me and the driver did a double take, and I was recognized a few other times, but for the most part I ran quietly. Nobody expected me to be back so soon. I went up to Freeport that afternoon and my front steps were littered with presents. I found a blueberry bush on my back steps, ready for planting. I'd also mentioned my chagrin over not putting up any strawberry jam that summer, so there was a lot of that, too. This was Maine's way of saying "We love you." The feeling was definitely mutual.

I was sorry to miss the closing ceremonies, but there was a wedding to plan and the invitations had to be ready for mailing in less than a month. I hadn't picked out my dress yet, and I was sure there would be a number of unexpected hitches. It seemed best to get my feet on the ground as soon as possible.

Portland was insistent about holding a parade. I really didn't look forward to the fuss, but it was to be an event for Maine's Olympians: Billy Swift, pitcher on the silver-medal baseball team; Holly Metcalf of Arrowsic, a member of the gold-medal women's rowing eight; and me. (At the Maine Sports Hall of Fame induction dinner I said that Billy's mother, who had fifteen children, should be recognized for her athletic prowess.)

I have to admit that I expected to be embarrassed. But when I saw the thousands of people who'd come out to see us I was touched. It was one of the nicest days of my life. People crowded around our cars to sling confetti at us and shake our hands. It took a long time to travel the half mile between Longfellow Square and Monument Square on Congress Street, but I didn't have to work to keep a smile plastered on my face. Later, my cheek muscles ached. Senators George Mitchell and William Cohen, Governor Joseph Brennan, and other state and city dignitaries awaited us at Monument Square. Senator Mitchell gave us each a flag that had flown over the U.S. Capitol and the three of us made short speeches.

From then on the honors stacked up almost faster than I could acknowledge them. The Maine Hall of Fame bent a rule and inducted me right away, even though one is not supposed to make it until five years after retirement.

My mother would call and tell me how many hours it had taken her to move through the supermarket that day, and we would go on to talk about some wedding detail. I was totally unable to settle down. I concentrated on staying on my feet until my wedding day.

On September 15 I won the Philadelphia Half-Marathon with a time of 1:08:31, a new world best. Adrenaline did it all; otherwise, I was running on fumes.

September 22 was Homecoming at Bowdoin. I was asked to help launch the college's capital fund drive during the football game by running into the end zone with President Roy Greason at halftime. As the *Bowdoin Alumnus* said in its Homecoming issue: "The president has since claimed he got there first." We carried a torch between us. Now *that* was embarrassing, but . . . anything for Alma Mater.

A week later Scott and I were married. Though we had five hundred guests, it was somehow a very intimate wedding. Everyone present had had a hand in our lives. After some shaky weather in the morning it turned into a beautiful day.

I may have been one of the few brides in history to enjoy her wedding reception as much as the guests did. I woke up positive that I didn't have the energy to make it through the day. But I marched into the church to "Chariots of Fire" and never looked back. Both of us smiled all day long—at each other, the guests, the sky, whatever. I was having such a good time saying hello to people at the reception that I didn't want to leave. Scott's only regret was that we heard so little of Schooner Fare, the folk trio that played. We changed the wedding date to accommodate their schedule, but we only really heard them play one song, while we were cutting the chocolate zucchini cake.

When we finally had to leave, as the sunlight was beginning to fail, Scott led me to the dock and we went up a few coves in the boat he'd built for me to a waiting car. Guests stood on the shore and threw birdseed at us. I wondered if fish would eat the birdseed.

We drove to Boston that evening so that we could catch a plane for Bermuda early the next morning. Scott only had a couple of days because he had just started business school. We barely made the plane and had to sit on either side of the aisle. If we had missed it we planned to go to Montreal—anything to remove ourselves from the utter chaos for a few days. We giggled about all the honeymoon couples and I'm sure they giggled about us—we were all so obvious. When the plane was airborne a flight attendant moved us into first class so that we could sit together. In Bermuda we slept for two days in the sun.

Once the wedding was over I was inundated with requests

for endorsements and appearances. As usual, I had difficulty saying no and drove myself to exhaustion. On November 17 I went to Chicago for the Rosemont Turkey Trot and did publicity for it all that day. I had no energy left the next day for the race and dropped out before it began. That made me feel awful; I'd always been treated well by the Rosemont people and didn't like to let them down. But I simply didn't have anything to give.

My life had been active before, but never to this extent. After my wedding I literally lived out of a suitcase until Christmas. I would wake up in the middle of the night and sit up to orient myself—I never really knew where I was. At year's end I was almost too tired to give thanks for everything that had happened. Almost.

I wanted time to reflect upon and enjoy the love I'd been shown. My first impulse was to try to repay everyone for every kindness; now I knew I needed some peace. I guessed, incorrectly, that peace was in the offing for 1985.

TEN

I have been asked why I wanted to run another marathon after the Olympics. In other words, "Isn't an Olympic gold medal enough for anybody?"

The answer is yes and no. There probably aren't many amateur athletes who don't dream of competing in the Olympic Games or imagine what it would be like to feel a gold medal slipped over their heads. That was my goal for many years, and when I achieved it I was thrilled. But I wasn't finished with my running career, because I had another goal: to run a marathon under two hours and twenty minutes. So, while the Olympic experience was everything I hoped it would be, it wasn't a natural stopping place for me. I still have a few miles to go.

The answer to the question was even simpler in 1985, when I was trying to pay back every favor I'd ever received, trying to enjoy married life with Scott, and trying to find thirty seconds for myself once in a while. I had to run another marathon because it would be the one thing that would make me continue to plan my day around my training. It might be the only way to get the peace I was after.

I was a long time learning my lesson, however. I started the year determined to spend time with Scott, since he had a vacation in January. Because he was in school and I was on the road, we'd seen little of each other since our wedding. So when *Ms.* magazine asked me to come to New York to accept a Woman of the Year award, I said no. Geraldine Ferraro, Cyndi Lauper, and Charity Grant, a ten-year-old who refused a reading prize from an all-male club, were among the other honorees. I was proud to be in their company but hated to break up the quiet time Scott and I had hoped for.

A few days before the awards ceremony someone from *Ms.* called while I was running and talked to Scott. The magazine needed some background information for Peter Ueberroth, who was going to accept the award for me. Well, I decided then that if Peter Ueberroth, whom I hold in high esteem, could find time in his schedule to accept the award, I could do as much. Scott agreed to go and we had a good time despite the change of plans.

After that my resolve weakened and I traveled much more than I wanted to. I went to New York again in February and was the official starter for the 3,000m race at the U.S. Olympic Invitational meet. I'd finished second in that race the two previous years, but my training wasn't going well and I don't like to compete if I'm not properly prepared. From January to April I was reduced to single workouts most days; if I ran doubles twice a week I was lucky. My mileage was down to seventy miles a week, and even those weren't satisfying, since they were so often run on unfamiliar roads away from home, where I couldn't measure my performance against past times. It was brutal to be out of Maine so much. When I have to travel I want to go somewhere, return to Maine, and then set out for the next destination. Even a day in Maine helps. But through the winter and spring of 1985 I made a number of road trips, whistle-stop affairs that kept me traveling farther and farther from home. I felt as if the cords that connected me to home were being stretched to impossible lengths, and any moment they would snap, leaving me stranded someplace, not knowing where I was. If Scott hadn't been his usual, understanding self, I think I'd have fallen apart. But he told me to do whatever I felt was right; he'd wait for things to settle down.

Reporters began to notice that I wasn't racing and assumed I was apathetic. They said I wasn't hungry enough, but that when I really wanted to run again, I'd shape up. I *was* hungry, though. I didn't run to become famous so I could show myself off around the world; I ran because I loved the sport. Cut off from the training loops I knew and loved, I was unable to make any headway. My mind was working every minute, trying to escape the physical lethargy brought on by travel and the demands on my time, but my body wouldn't cooperate. I wanted to get back to racing more than I had ever wanted anything. I saw several doctors, hoping they could pinpoint a physical deficiency. I had blood tests, an endocrinologic workup, and other exams; I was found to be borderline anemic again, but there was nothing drastically wrong. I needed to be home, resting my head. I vowed to stop traveling in late spring when Scott got out of school for the summer.

In the meantime I received stacks of mail and hundreds of requests to appear at dinners and career days and the like. Charities wanted me on their boards, or at least a public service announcement for their cause. My lawyer, Ed Whittemore, and the staff at Athletics West handled many of these requests, but I still had loads of mail at home to deal with. The people who made their appeals directly to me suffered most. I would read their messages, promise myself to make a decision one way or another, and then put the letters into growing piles. If I let something hang for too long I'd get a registered letter asking why I hadn't responded; I felt I was being pulled out of shape.

Finally I decided to organize my mail hierarchically: first, charities that meant something to me, then letters from kids, then letters from people with physical problems, and, last, requests from civic groups. I needed that overall structure to cope, even as badly as I was coping.

Virtually all of the charities were worthy, but I knew I could dilute my message by agreeing to represent too many causes, so I often had to say no. I hoped that people would realize I was doing as much as I could, but there were those who would say, "Oh, it's *terrible* that you don't have a minute's peace. Now, how about coming to our banquet for an award?" All of a sudden there seemed to be an award for everything. It was easier to refuse an award than it was to say no to a charity, but the award givers were the hardest to shake.

I cut down the charity list as the winter progressed and finally settled on a handful to represent: the Multiple Sclerosis Society, because a friend's father was stricken with that disease; Special Olympics, a natural; Mothers Against Drunk Driving; and the Maine Lung Association. Bowdoin asked for my help in a number of ways and I was glad to give it, and there were some state and civic duties I didn't mind assuming, but by summer my life was considerably less hectic. I learned that the best way to make a contribution to a cause is to determine what you want to do and then seek out the proper organization. Lately I haven't been waiting for them to get sick of asking me. The Gulf of Maine Aquarium, Bowdoin, and the Recreation-Liaison Committee in Freeport had to ask only once. I said yes to each because I knew I could make a long-term contribution. I don't want to be a human Band-Aid anymore, rushing to a studio for a quick public service announcement for a cause that doesn't grab me. I've chosen to use my influence where I think it will do the most good. For instance, I started working on a special project, "Joanie's Jam for Sam," to honor the late Samantha Smith, the Maine teenager who was invited to visit the Soviet Union by Yuri Andropov, because I respected Samantha so much.

All in all, however, the winter of 1985 dragged me out. I missed Scott and my training regimen.

In March I was emotionally drained after winning the Bowdoin Prize, an award given once every five years to the alumnus who has made the most significant contribution in his or her field. I was bowled over by it; but I wrote and gave a speech, and after that was as organized and calm as a split wire. Through it all, Maine was running to cold and mud, so I took off to compete in the Jacksonville River Run in an uncharacteristic search for warmth.

I thought I was ready to run fast in Florida. My training had picked up slightly in early March and I figured I had enough momentum to win a race. But, though I ran a time that wasn't too far over my personal best, I finished sixth. I beat myself all the way home and hit the roads hard for a couple of days. Nothing seemed to work.

On April 22 I went to the post office for my mail and the postman said, "Now what are you going to do?" About what, I wanted to know. "Ingrid Kristiansen set a new marathon record in London," he said. Her time was 2:21:06. That did motivate me a little, but I still felt flat.

In early May I was satisfied, but not pleased, with my winning time in the Old Kent River Bank run. Then in San Francisco I ran very well, establishing a new record at the

Examiner Bay-To-Breakers race, even though somebody brought a mule on the course and screwed up my rhythm— try running sometime with hooves clop-clop-clopping in your ears. I blew by the mule after a short time, though, and, more important, I beat the Aggies, a local running club. Before the race they boasted that their centipede (a perennial feature of this "fun run") had never been beaten by a woman. They said they weren't scared of me. People shouldn't say such things: it's like putting on a pair of spangled trousers and yelling "Toro!" Not only did I beat them, I really enjoyed beating them.

I then ran my worst race of the year, in the L'eggs Mini. A dear friend was being married in Maine that day, so the New York Road Runners Club provided a private airplane to get me back home in time for the wedding. But I wished I hadn't agreed to run.

Scott came to New York the day before, and when he was dressing the next morning I said, from under the covers, "Scott, do you have any idea where I'm going to finish today?" He usually has a good sense of how I'll do in a race. Normally he'll say, "Oh, you're going to win," or "You'll place in the top three." That morning, he leaned over and whispered in my ear, "I know exactly where you're going to finish."

I said, "Where?"

"At the finish line."

Scott was right; that's where I finished. I came dragging over the line in eleventh place. If someone had handed me a pledge saying I'd never run again, I might have signed it. I had never gone as long as ten months feeling so uncertain about my career. I was beginning to wonder if I'd ever feel right again.

At least it was summer and Scott was out of school. I made

good on my promise to stop traveling so much. Little by little, things began to snap into place. The anger I felt in New York did me some good; I used it in my training. I was able to plan my day around my running because I was in comfortable territory; and, though I was busy, I was busy at home. That made all the difference.

Scott restored the barn while I picked berries, saw friends, worked in the garden, and ran. It all took me back to earlier days in Cape Elizabeth when I could spend whole afternoons lazing on a beach without worrying about which cause or individual I was slighting. I realized I couldn't allow my celebrity to exact that sort of toll ever again.

My training improved immensely over the summer, but my heels returned to haunt me. Sometimes I had to stop on a run because one heel wouldn't make the right moves. I had twinges and burning, pulsating sensations, as if hot liquid were squirting all over the inside of my foot. Dr. Leach injected the heels with cortisone. As long as they functioned I didn't want to ease up on my training. I was running over a hundred miles a week and feeling better about my physical conditioning than I had since the previous August. Though I was a bit skeptical about my condition and half expected everything to blow up in my face, I wanted to keep going for as long as I possibly could. I'd told the runners at B.U. to let pain be their guide, so you can add me to the list of people who don't practice what they preach. Pain didn't mean anything to me if my physical and mental conditions were, on balance, improving. Pain counted only when it managed to stop my forward movement.

I was working very hard at my training in hopes of improving on my mediocre spring and early summer results. The Bix 7 in Iowa on July 27 would be the first opportunity to assess the results of my new regimen. I needed a good race to give me the momentum to carry me through to the Chicago Marathon, where I hoped to break Ingrid Kristiansen's marathon mark.

I was asked by Falmouth officials in the spring to commit to run there; I told them how I was feeling and assured them that they wouldn't want me if I hadn't improved by August. They got in touch with me the weekend before the race and I still couldn't make up my mind whether I was ready to take the big step Falmouth represented. I said I'd call back on Wednesday, but I put it off, so they phoned again on Thursday morning. That evening I told them I'd definitely be there. I thought I might as well run where I was loved. And I had a terrific race, setting a new course record, taking four seconds off my previous mark, and winning Falmouth for the sixth time.

After that I ran another winning half-marathon in Philadelphia on September 18, and I knew I was ready for a marathon. My plan was to run in Chicago or New York, and it was soon clear that the best competition would be in Chicago. Ingrid Kristiansen and Rosa Mota chose that race, so I did too. I love competing against Ingrid, and she feels the same way about me. According to *Sports Illustrated*, the treadmill in her basement faces a mirror and a photograph of me winning the 1983 Boston Marathon.

I ran 120-mile weeks through September and my times were faster than ever. I was in the best shape of my life, barring the period immediately preceding my knee problems. My heels were sore and inflamed, but I discussed this problem only with Scott, Dr. Leach, Bob Sevene, Ed Whittemore, and Susan Hughes. If my heels stopped me in Chicago, they stopped me. I didn't want excuses made if I had a bad race.

Thinking Chicago could be my last marathon, I invited Sev, Susan Hughes and Paul Surface, Ed and Janice Whittemore, and my parents to be there, even though I was worried about functioning in such a gang. My parents don't understand why I space out before a big race, and sometimes, without realizing it, I'll say something that hurts them.

I went running with Scott on Saturday morning and my heart sank. I'd been hoping for a day such as the one New York enjoyed for its marathon the following week: warm, bright, and sunny. But it was windy and gray in Chicago all weekend, and I felt dreary. Saturday night I hardly slept. In the minutes before dawn I had a variation on my usual pre-race dream. This time I was walking with Ingrid Kristiansen to the starting line when I realized that I desperately needed to get to a bathroom. I said, "Wait here, Ingrid. I'll come get you and we'll go on together." I left her on a street corner. While I was in the john I heard the race announcer call for us to line up and I ran to join the pack, assuming Ingrid had gotten into line in my absence. But when the race started I saw Ingrid, still standing on the sidewalk where I'd left her. I yelled, "Come on, just jump in. Nobody will notice." Ingrid asked if I was sure she wouldn't be disqualified and I said yes, I was sure. But I knew somebody would see her if she tried, so I turned around, faced the pack, and screamed, "Hold it! We have to start all over again." Then I woke: I didn't know what to make of the dream.

Sunday was dim and muggy. Sev told me the wind would die down before it mattered, but that didn't make me feel much better. He and Scott and I took a cab to a point a few blocks away from the starting line and walked from there. I jogged a little and stretched, trying to get warm, while Scott made sure I had the right shoes and socks and other equipment. As always, these were the worst moments; I was dying to get it over with. I had to go to the bathroom, but the line in front of the porta-potties was hundreds of people long.

Patricia Owens, a friend from New York who has been involved with helping runners for several years, had come out from the East to see the race. Without hesitation she took me by the hand and led me to the front of the line. "Excuse me," she said to a man who was waiting, "this is Joan Benoit Samuelson. Could she get in there ahead of you?" He said "Yeah, of course!" and I felt stupid, but thanked goodness for Patricia.

It was a fast race, especially through the first ten miles. Ingrid was on my shoulder from the beginning, leeching my concentration by making me wonder what she was up to. I kept expecting her to pass and leave me behind; Ingrid is famous for her fast starts and kick. But she just stayed there, right by me, for the first twenty miles. She almost broke my spirit. I was apathetic at the start of the race because of the weather and had written the race off when I realized I wouldn't be able to break 2:20 on such a day. My low hung on for the first fifteen miles as Ingrid relentlessly made me take the pace. The pressure lifted only once, when Ingrid offered me her water bottle.

"What's in it besides water?" I asked.

"Salt," Ingrid said.

"Salt? No *thanks*!"

"No, no," she said, giggling. "Shoo-gar." We laughed, but soon we were back to business.

When we passed the fifteen-mile mark, I figured Ingrid's strategy was working; she was wearing me out to the point where I wished she'd go by me and end the misery. But she didn't go. If she had kicked away then, I'd have settled for second. Five more miles. I couldn't keep on this way to the end, so I decided to try to get rid of her one way or another. I opened my stride as far as I could and moved out. I ran a 5:30 mile between miles twenty and twenty-one, on an incline, and Ingrid dropped back for good. I went on to win the race with a new American best of 2:21:21. I hadn't reached my goal, but I was happy with the race because I'd come back from a bout of apathy to win. I proved I could run effectively again in a long, grueling, competitive marathon. If I was mildly disappointed with my time, it was only because I had thought this might be my last marathon. It's hard to gear up to such a high pitch, only to find that you must try again another time.

That is, quite literally, the story of my life. I think all athletes who strive for excellence share the same story.

I was born with both a competitive drive and a sense of adventure. These two characteristics combined to keep me on the ski slopes in storms when I was a child, they helped me face unpleasant jobs, and they forced me to set running goals that I had to attain. I couldn't run another marathon without my competitive spirit—the training and the race itself take too much of a toll on the body to continue if the results aren't there. If I'd never won a marathon I think my heart would have broken years ago. I love to run—it will always be part of my life—but I would never have come this far without the need to best my competition.

My sense of adventure has taken me into unknown territory since the Chicago race. I waited for the emotional letdown to come in December or January, and in the meantime Dr. Leach operated on my heels again. But the letdown never arrived. From the day after that race I have felt driven to stay in top condition—hence the swimming, bicycling, and weight lifting when my feet were healing. I've got all the energy in the world. And I know why—my goal is still out there.

I think 2:20 will be broken soon and I'd like to be the one to do it. It's a psychological as well as a physical barrier; the woman who breaks it will undoubtably usher in a new age in the sport of running, the way Roger Bannister did when he shattered the four-minute mile. My desire to make this watershed is akin to the adventurer's need to explore unknown ground. Whether or not I can achieve this goal, I have to try.

I wasn't ready to run the Boston Marathon in 1986, so I prepared myself to watch Ingrid Kristiansen break 2:20 and take this obsession away from me. She didn't, but because I had resolved that she would, my feelings of relentless pursuit softened. Now, if someone else gets there before me I'll be disappointed, but I won't quit running marathons until I've given my best shot in pursuit of a sub-2:20.

Maybe I should say that's when I'll limp away. I can't walk properly unless I'm wearing shoes, and it's possible that I'll never be able to do so again. After the Chicago Marathon I didn't run another competitive race until the Boston Milk Run on April 13, 1986, because I wasn't training effectively— I couldn't bring my heels around fast enough to create a sure, comfortable stride.

I had been taking anti-inflammatory drugs in order to get through Falmouth—assuring myself I would stop the medication after the race. But I finished a disappointing seventh; the drugs seemed to dehydrate me the day before, which is the worst thing that can happen in a race notorious for being run in high humidity. Realizing that it made no sense to mask my pain with anti-inflammatories, I decided to cut my training considerably to see if my heel would quiet down and I could run in the Philadelphia Half-Marathon in September. But the week before Philadelphia I knew I would have a hard time covering the course, let alone being competitive. It was at this time that I knew the Chicago Marathon was out of the question. It was the first year since 1979 that I hadn't run at least one marathon.

When I faced heel surgery after the 1985 Chicago Marathon, I thought I was in the best shape of my life. Not wanting to lose that edge, I probably rushed my training. Although I was able to set new American records for 25 kilometers and 10 miles that spring, I was unable to put in the necessary training to run in the Boston Marathon. Having run close to a personal best (31:58) in a 10k race in Green Bay, Wisconsin, in June, I was motivated to increase my mileage for Chicago. But in the Bix 7 in late July, my heel flared up on the hilly course, and I knew I had perhaps pushed myself too hard and my fall marathon plans looked bleak.

All of a sudden I began to question whether I would be able to run five miles a decade from now. The soreness and tightness I felt every day gave me real concern. I knew that if I literally ran myself into the ground, I wouldn't be able to run for pleasure in later life. I've seen too many ex-athletes hobbling around the banquet circuit to be unaware of the grim possibilities that could lie ahead. Every step I take pushes me further into the mystery.

Nike certainly is aware of my desire to continue competitive running. They have gone out of their way to make shoes that will enable me to train and run hard. There are certain things I look for in a shoe. I like a heavy, straight-lasted shoe with a supportive heel center and mid-sole. I also want some flexibility in the forefoot. However, what I like and what I think works best for me might be damaging for someone else. We all have different feet, and thus different requirements. There is no "best" shoe. There is a large variety of different footwear on the market to accommodate most everyone's needs, and my main advice in the matter is that each runner should take time to select the proper shoe. Nike also gives me any research findings that might help my particular problem.

I haven't given up, fear or no fear; I hope that my good training techniques will return. Sticking to my goal as long as I can is important. It may sound simplistic, but I have faith in medicine; I believe a new procedure will soon make it possible for me to dance on my fortieth birthday without a limp. I figure if I do my job and am the best athlete I can be, some doctor will do his or her job and develop a new treatment to repair the damage I do to myself.

Faith is the key to everything. That's what I tell people who say I have helped them. My open letter to them would be brief: Don't lose sight of your goals. No matter what the obstacles are, don't let anything deter you from your best effort. Don't allow anyone to tell you what you can and cannot do. Be tough, be stubborn, love yourself, and find friends who believe in you. Most of all, recognize your victories: don't thank someone else when you bear up under chemotherapy; thank yourself. It was your pain and you withstood it. If you must learn something from me, let it be that. Love yourself—not hedonistically, but essentially. Love what you are, protect your dreams, and develop your talents to their fullest extent.

Kenny Moore had some interesting things to say about our sport in his 1986 *Sports Illustrated* profile of Ingrid Kristiansen: "The three best female marathoners ever, Kristiansen, Waitz and Benoit Samuelson, all are models of stability, wit and integrity. The parallels are striking, and not coincidental. All are happily married. All are aware of their own compulsiveness and are able to keep it within healthy bounds. All have serious interests outside their running. (And all, as it happens, ski.) It has to be this way. Inevitably, those best at the marathon, this event that defines lasting it out, lead lives of balance. They have outlasted runners of comparable talent, who destroyed it one way or another, through overtraining, overracing, dumb tactics or perfectionist burnout."

The time is coming when I will have to move on to other things. I've been running in circles for ten years. My career has shown me the world and given me opportunities I might never have enjoyed if I hadn't been a runner. Whatever I choose to do with the rest of my life, my running has taught me that I can reach almost any goal if I want it enough. My inclination, once my final objective is reached (or I make the final attempt at it), may be to help others, but I'm sure there will be secret, selfish ambitions for me as well. At the moment I am in the world's debt, so I see an immediate future filled with efforts to square the accounts.

If I limp into that future on sore heels, so be it. Maybe I'll reach my last running goal after all; maybe I won't. But no matter what happens, I will carry the lessons I have learned— of perseverance, humor, friendship, and hard work—with me. So the idea of having no further milestones to reach in running doesn't upset me. I've never been just a runner; with my family, friends, college, and home state defining me otherwise, I could never be that.

There will always be something to strive for. My hope is for the heart to strive forever.

A NOTE ON THE TYPE

The text of this book was set by CRT in Janson, a film version of
a typeface thought to have been made by the Dutchman Anton
Janson, who was a practicing typefounder in Leipzig during the
years 1668–1687. However, it has been conclusively demon-
strated that these types are actually the work of Nicholas Kis
(1650–1702), a Hungarian, who most probably learned his trade
from the master Dutch typefounder Dirk Voskens. The type is
an example of the influential and sturdy Dutch types that pre-
vailed in England up to the time William Caslon developed his
own designs from them.

Composed by American–Stratford Graphic
Services, Inc.,
Brattleboro, Vermont
Printed and bound by The Haddon Craftsmen, Inc.,
Scranton, Pennsylvania

Designed by Julie Duquet